KOMBUCHA, KEFIR, AND BEYOND

KOMBUCHA, KEFIR, AND BEYOND

**ALEX LEWIN &
RAQUEL GUAJARDO**

A FUN &
FLAVORFUL
GUIDE TO
FERMENTING
your own
PROBIOTIC
BEVERAGES
at home

FAIR WINDS

© 2017 Quarto Publishing Group USA Inc.
Text © 2017 Alex Lewin and Raquel Guajardo
Photography © 2017 Quarto Publishing Group USA Inc.

First Published in 2017 by Fair Winds Press, an imprint of The Quarto Group,
100 Cummings Center, Suite 265-D, Beverly, MA 01915, USA.
T (978) 282-9590 F (978) 283-2742 QuartoKnows.com

Fair Winds Press titles are also available at discount for retail, wholesale, promotional, and bulk purchase. For details, contact the Special Sales Manager by email at specialsales@quarto.com or by mail at The Quarto Group, Attn: Special Sales Manager, 401 Second Avenue North, Suite 310, Minneapolis, MN 55401, USA.

21 20 19 18 17   1 2 3 4 5
ISBN: 978-1-59233-738-5

Digital edition published in 2017

Library of Congress Cataloging-in-Publication Data is available.

Cover and book design: Stacy Wakefield Forte
Photography: Nader Khouri
Food and prop styling: Leila Nichols

Printed and bound in China.

TO THE ANCESTORS AND
TRADITIONS OF MEXICO AND
THE UNITED STATES, AND TO
WORKING TOGETHER.

—————————————————

AND TO INDIGENOUS PEOPLES
EVERYWHERE—MAY WE ALL
GROK YOUR WISDOM BEFORE
IT'S TOO LATE.

PREFACES
PAGE 8

CONTENTS

1
WHY FERMENT
YOUR DRINKS?
PAGE 10

2
OUR CULTURED
HISTORY
PAGE 26

3
FERMENTATION,
SCIENCE, AND
HEALTH
PAGE 34

4
BEFORE YOU
START
PAGE 46

5
FIVE-MINUTE
RECIPES
PAGE 66

6
STARTERS,
MASTER RECIPES,
AND GENERAL
PRINCIPLES
PAGE 76

7
KOMBUCHA
AND JUN
PAGE 98

8
VEGETABLE
DRINKS
PAGE 116

9
SODAS
PAGE 126

10
BEERS, GRAINS,
AND ROOTS
PAGE 138

11
WINES, CIDERS,
AND FRUITS
(AND VINEGAR!)
PAGE 152

12
MEXICAN
PRE-HISPANIC
DRINKS
PAGE 170

13
FERMENTED
COCKTAILS
PAGE 182

RESOURCES
PAGE 200

ABOUT THE AUTHORS
PAGE 202

ACKNOWLEDGMENTS
PAGE 203

RECIPE DIRECTORY
PAGE 204

INDEX
PAGE 206

RAQUEL GUAJARDO

I WAS BORN and raised in Monterrey, Nuevo León, an industrial town surrounded by mountains in the north of Mexico that is well known for its carne asada, cabrito, tortilla de harina, and beer. As a proud regiomontana, I have always loved beer, but I didn't associate it with fermentation, and never in my wildest dreams could I have imagined myself brewing my own.

For me, fermentation started in Seattle, Washington, during a Real Food Cooking Course taught by Monica Corrado. Among other things, she taught me how to make sauerkraut and the principles of fermentation. She recommended the book *Wild Fermentation* by Sandor Katz, and soon I was hooked on everything fermented.

Then, two years ago, I invited Sandor to teach a workshop in Monterrey. More people got hooked, and I got inspired to experiment and come up with my own recipes.

Then I invited Alex to teach another fermentation workshop in Monterrey, on kimchi and the science of fermentation. During his stay, he tasted a couple of my fermented beverages, and I am pretty sure he enjoyed them. After all, the idea for this book was born in my kitchen as we drank pulque and tepache.

ALEX LEWIN

I GREW UP in the Northeast of the U.S., in New York, Connecticut, and Massachusetts. I started thinking and reading about food and health when I was in my 20s. One book would say one thing, another book would say something different and incompatible, and both would have good justifications for what they said. I was curious by nature, and at the time I hated unsolved mysteries, so I started reading more. This led me on a path of discovery informed by Andrew Weil, Sandor Katz, Sally Fallon, the Institute for Integrative Nutrition, the Cambridge School of Culinary Arts, and many more. In fact, my views are informed by almost everyone I talk with about health and food. And I have made my peace with unsolved mysteries—there will always be some things that we don't know, and I'm okay with that. Fermentation, especially with wild starters, depending as it does on invisible forces and serendipity, is a great stage on which to dance with the unknown.

I speak for both Raquel and myself when I say that we've enjoyed being learning partners together. Our skills and perspectives and communities are similar in so many ways, and complementary in so many others; working together has been fun and enlightening.

We are all stronger when we work together, embracing difference, diversity, the unfamiliar, and the unknown. Do not let misguided demagogues suggest otherwise.

We hope that you enjoy this book that we've brewed up for you. Salud!

WHY FERMENT YOUR DRINKS?

CHAPTER ONE

We are in the midst of a health crisis—or, to put it another way, a disease crisis. For proof, just turn on the television. You'll be exhorted to buy diabetes maintenance equipment; cholesterol-lowering drugs with significant side effects; digestive nostrums that blunt unpleasant symptoms without addressing underlying causes; allergy pills that suppress the immune system; painkillers; and more.

The interspersed commercials are for sugary drinks, junk food, and toxic personal care and cleaning products, the use of which likely contributes to conditions such as diabetes, cardiovascular disease, digestive problems, and allergies. Sound familiar? It doesn't seem like this is a complete coincidence.

Love it or hate it, advertising is a reliable bellwether: The commercials we see are the ones that sell product and make money. Super Bowl commercials, for example, are the caviar of the domestic advertising world. Guaranteed millions of viewers, these ads cost 10 million dollars per minute. Yet during the 2016 Super Bowl, we saw an ad for a drug to address a very specific malady that many of us had never considered: opioid-induced constipation. Opioids are opium-derived and opium-related drugs, including a long list of prescription painkillers and street drugs. If we were a nation of healthy people, we'd be seeing different commercials.

Mexico finds itself in the same boat as the United States. It is one of the world's most obese countries with one of the highest infant diabetes rates. American fast food chains and supermarkets have been crowding out *mercados*, where fresh seasonal food used to be found. For the younger generations, buying American fast food is part of the modern way of life, cool and hip, like having a cell phone, whereas the typical grandma foods such as pozole, tamales, and mole are old-fashioned. Even the tortilla, the hallmark of Mexican food, has changed for the worse, and sadly, traditional *tortillerías* are disappearing.

As the United States goes, so go not only her American neighbors, but much of the world. With the expansion of markets for big-business food and tobacco products comes diabetes, heart disease, obesity, cancer, and chronic digestive and immune system dysfunction. And these maladies create new markets for pharmaceutical products.

Are drugs really the best way to break this cycle? Maybe fermented beverages can help.

WHAT IS FERMENTATION, ANYWAY?

Fermentation is the transformation of food through the action of microbes. Microbes are microscopic life forms, including bacteria, yeasts, and molds. (Viruses are sometimes considered microbes. They have no metabolism, so they aren't direct agents of fermentation, and they won't be discussed here.) Via chemical reactions, these microbes transform carbohydrates (sugars and starches) into acids, alcohols, and gases. Along the way, small but useful amounts of vitamins and enzymes are created too.

Digestion refers to processes in living organisms that break down food into various components. Digestion is generally accelerated by heat and catalyzed by special proteins called enzymes. Enzymes are employed by all life forms, from microbes to mammals. In fact, it turns out that many of the same enzymes used by microbes are also found in the human digestive

tract. This is not a coincidence—many of our gut enzymes are created by microbes that live there. These enzymes play a crucial role in human digestion.

These enzymes also play a crucial role in fermentation, which happens when microbes use them to start breaking down food. These microbes are effectively predigesting our fermenting food, in some of the same ways that we ourselves digest food inside our bodies, using some of the same enzymes. So when we eat fermented foods, we are getting ahead of the game; these foods are easier for our bodies to digest. This may help us to better assimilate important nutrients from the food—we have more time to break down compounds that could inhibit nutrient uptake. It may also reduce difficult-to-digest and inflammatory compounds, so we face fewer signs of digestive difficulties such as gas, bloating, acid reflux, and heartburn. This helps us to mitigate, avoid, and sometimes reverse chronic long-term digestive diseases.

As by-products of metabolism and digestion, some microbes create meaningful amounts of B and C vitamins. Some microbes also create other, more obscure human nutrients, including some whose functions we are still learning about and some that we may never know about or understand. Additionally, many of the products of fermentation promote health, stave off disease, and/or actively reverse some types of health problems in humans and other bigger creatures. This is particularly the case when small amounts of minerals or organic materials, such as herbs, are included in the fermenting process. We are only beginning to understand some of the substances and mechanisms involved.

EAT REAL FOODS

Food science does not necessarily prioritize the discovery of new food nutrients—there's much more incentive to invent new industrial processes that save time and money, or to create new flavorings for potato chips and fast food. From the point of view of human health, food science advances slowly, sometimes taking two steps forward and one step back. Unfortunately, that means the messages that reach consumers about what they should or shouldn't eat may not be focused on what would help them maintain robust health.

Because food science isn't focused on nutrition, it's worth our while to seek out real foods—foods that are close in form to how they occur in nature, processed in the home kitchen, with trace compounds intact. Industrially processed foods almost always lose nutritional value during processing; even if they look okay on paper, they are often stripped of poorly understood or unknown trace compounds. Their production process serves the food producers first and the public second or third or not at all.

Consider the story of Soylent: In 2013, a pair of young entrepreneurs were creating tech products that they hoped would change the world. Because they wanted to maximize the time they spent working on their projects, they were frustrated that it took so long to select, procure, prepare, and eat food. So they applied their considerable analytic skills to the problem of food, and after researching modern dietary science, they came up with a formula for a meal replacement that included all known essential nutrients, in amounts and proportions consistent with the recommendations of the experts. Their goal was to create an "adult formula" that people could consume exclusively and indefinitely. Their friends were naturally curious about what they were doing and why they never wanted to share meals any more. Interest increased, and soon they formed a new company to sell the meal replacement, which they called Soylent. They've been selling Soylent ever since, and they've also expanded their company mission to include feeding people in need, in the United States and around the world.

They get full points for their social mission. They can help a lot of hungry people with Soylent. It is surely effective as a short-term or emergency meal replacement for people without access to food. But as a long-term meal replacement? It's doubtful that current dietary science knows everything there is to know about the nutrients that humans need to thrive. It seems likely that, 50 years from now, we will look back and think, "I can't believe they didn't know to include vitamin Z!" or something along those lines.

The early twentieth century saw huge advances in nutrition, with new nutrients being discovered quite often; since then, the rate of advancement has slowed a lot, which could lead one to believe that we are approaching full understanding. But often, when we think that we

WHAT'S IN A NAME?

The name *soylent* is a reference to a food product in the science fiction novel *Make Room! Make Room!* and to its better-known movie adaptation *Soylent Green*. In both the book and the movie, global overpopulation and climate change lead to miserable conditions on Earth, and most of the population are surviving on fully industrialized food rations, initially made of a combination of soy and lentils (soy-lent). In the movie, the food situation gets more dire, and the soylent formula undergoes several revisions; at the end, it is revealed that the latest version of this food, Soylent Green, contains an unexpected and shocking ingredient.

Whatever the (real) company's intention in associating itself with this story, it was a great marketing move—it got them a lot of attention.

INDUSTRIAL FOOD: CAVEAT EMPTOR

Dietary guidelines change over the years. This is partly because science progresses and our understanding of human health evolves. But the changes are not always moving us in the direction of increased health. Marketers, regulators, and even scientists all have their own agendas that are not always aligned with the advancement of truth or with the interests of people who eat food.

A marketer's priority, for instance, is to increase sales of his or her products. There are some limits, of course; if a product harms or kills customers, for instance, it could lead to a damaged reputation, expensive lawsuits, and/or regulatory action from government agencies. These negatives must be weighed against the positives of increased sales. A company's desired image plays a role in determining where the balance lies. Some companies depend on being known for healthy products and stewardship of the earth to help drive their sales. Others may focus more on operational efficiencies that help them sell at a lower price than their competition. Still others may focus on clever advertising (for example, breakfast cereals with cartoon characters) to drive sales. In any case, companies that wish to survive must try to convince people to buy their products. Regardless of long-term health benefits or detriments, their marketing message is always some version of "you should eat this."

Regulators must strike a balance between protecting citizens and enabling commerce. Regulations necessarily change slowly, more slowly than our understanding of human health evolves—if regulations changed every time a new study came out, it would be impossible for big companies to create viable multiyear business plans. And in the United States at least, many government regulators come from the industries that they regulate and may hope to return to those industries after they're done. This may motivate some of them to

finally understand a field of science completely, we get a rude awakening a few years (or a few decades) later. Just for example, in the 1890s, a respected physicist named Albert Abraham Michelson said, "most of the grand underlying principles [of physics] have been firmly established," and declared that all that remained was increasing the precision of measurements. Ten years later, the world of physics was shaken to its core by Albert Einstein and relativity, then again not too long after by Max Planck and quantum physics. Physics today has many more open questions than it did 120 years ago!

Human nutrition is even harder to study than physics. Conditions are harder to control, good experiments are harder to design, and experiments sometimes take decades from conception to start to finish. And ethical concerns make

16

favor their once-and-future corporate employers, meaning that their incentives may not be aligned with those of the people they are charged to protect.

Even scientists' choices and work are not motivated exclusively by the pursuit of pure and abstract truth or by solving the most important problems of the day. For one, the ability of scientists to research at all is constrained by the availability of money. If no one wants to fund a study, the study won't happen. Today, more and more research is underwritten not by universities or government grants but by corporations, whose choices are often guided by their desire to make money.

That's simply how market capitalism works. Additionally, sometimes scientists build their reputations around particular ideas that they create or support over decades. They may be reluctant to change their stated beliefs, beliefs around which they've built their careers, even when faced with new, compelling evidence that runs against their paradigms. We have seen this repeatedly over the years with the rise and fall of low-fat diets, transfats, various artificial sweeteners, mercury fillings, leaded gasoline and paint, cigarettes, and the like.

The principle of *caveat emptor*, "let the buyer beware," applies very much when it comes to food, despite the many well-meaning producers and regulators.

NOTE: *Caveat emptor* applies at least as much or more to personal care products, which are regulated less strictly than food. We administer most of them directly to the human body's largest organ—the skin—and they are absorbed quickly. Some of the compounds that can be found in personal care products include lead, mercury, arsenic, and hydrogenated cottonseed oil. See www.safecosmetics.org for more information.

human experiments more complicated than other sorts of experiments—you can't in good conscience experiment on a human the way you can on an atom, or even a rat. So it seems extremely unlikely that human nutrition is a "solved" field.

What mineral or vitamin cofactor might be missing from Soylent, and what might be the long-term effects of eating only synthetic food?

If you feel confident that we know everything there is to know about nutrients, and that you can get all of them from a manufactured powder, then feel free to bet your life on it! Otherwise, you might consider including traditional food in your diet, the kind that has seen human populations survive and often thrive for millennia and that contains nutrients that we don't yet know about. Human populations a thousand years ago had health challenges, to be sure, but they didn't have the particular problems that we have now, on the scale that we have them, even taking into account the changes in average lifespan.

WHAT ARE THE BENEFITS?

Fermented foods are usually either acidic (sour, low pH), alcoholic (slightly to moderately), or both. And pathogenic (sickness-inducing) microbes generally cannot survive in acidic or alcoholic environments. Thus, during the many times throughout history when getting safe drinking water has been a challenge, fermented drinks have been lifesavers, literally. But the benefits don't end there.

FERMENTED FOODS DON'T SPOIL QUICKLY.

The same factors that make fermented drinks safer than water—resistance to "bad" microbes—also help make them less prone to spoilage than unfermented foods and drinks. Fermentation can be a great way to prolong the useable life of foods when access to refrigeration is limited or nonexistent.

THEY'RE GOOD FOR YOU.

Even when access to safe drinking water is not an issue, fermented foods and drinks are important for people with challenged digestion. Many of the acids in fermented foods have pos-

itive health effects beyond their ability to keep the bad guys at bay: They can help resolve digestive disorders related to the regulation of stomach acid, such as acid reflux; They can also help smooth out blood sugar fluctuations. And small to moderate amounts of alcohol can have other health benefits for some people, including reduced risk of cardiovascular problems, relief of stress, and so on. For more on the health benefits of fermented drinks, see page 42.

HOME-FERMENTED DRINKS CAN BE LOWER IN ALCOHOL.

Large-scale modern alcohol production uses yeasts (microbes) that have been selectively bred for their ability to tolerate and produce high levels of alcohol. On the horizon are genetically-modified (GMO) yeasts, which would allow quicker and easier customization of yeasts with particular characteristics, including still higher alcohol tolerance, for use in industrial food and beverage production.

By contrast, small-scale and nonindustrial alcoholic fermentation often uses wild yeasts or yeasts that are not far from wild. These yeasts have a lower tolerance for alcohol than engineered yeasts, so the drinks they produce generally contain less alcohol, making them more suitable for more frequent consumption, in larger quantities, and by more sensitive groups of people (children, the elderly, the infirm, and pregnant women). Daily consumption of low-alcohol beverages has been the norm in many places and at many times throughout history, especially when and where it was hard to get

18

safe drinking water. This has been true even in religious communities that today are generally opposed to the use of alcohol by their members. Mormons, for instance, had more relaxed rules around alcohol until the early 1900s, when the production and sale of alcohol were prohibited entirely in the United States. And the idea that Islam forbids the consumption of alcohol is an oversimplification; it depends whom you ask. What is more clear is that it forbids drunkenness. Consider that kefir, a fermented milk drink, is said to have been a gift from Mohammed to his people: Kefir contains sometimes noticeable amounts of alcohol. And for what it's worth, the word *alcohol* comes from Arabic. Having said all of that, alcohol consumption is a more complicated topic today in car-centric societies because many of us are expected to be able to regularly pilot two-ton rolling fortresses flawlessly at 100+ feet per second!

THEY SUPPORT THE MICROBES IN YOUR GUT.

The microbes that are instrumental in the transformation of live fermented foods can also help reestablish a healthy, balanced microbial ecosystem in your gut. Gut microbes play roles in many important body processes, including digestion, the endocrine system, the immune system, and the regulation of blood cholesterol levels. Ingesting microbe-rich food ushers these potential settlers toward the gut.

Preindustrial humans generally did not have a shortage of microbes in their diet, although they did sometimes get sick from the wrong ones. By contrast, industrial humans eat a lot of processed, canned, and cooked foods—one aspect of what has been called the Standard American Diet (SAD)—and not very many raw or fermented foods. Supplementing these diets with some fermented foods can provide us with the missing "nutrient" of microbes.

It is worth mentioning that most cells within the boundaries of the human body are not human cells at all, but are microbes of one sort or another. A great deal of this microbial diversity exists within our digestive tracts. And if we look at the diversity of genetic material, we find that microbes dominate the human organism: One estimate is that 99% of the distinct DNA contained inside a typical human is from microbes! So by the numbers, at least, humans are not individual beings at all, but rather heterogeneous communities of cells of various species—or to be less technical, great skin-bags of invisible creatures, with a lot of coming and going. These species are crucial to the proper functioning of our bodies—also known as our health.

We are ecosystems, and what we perceive as our health is hard or impossible to separate from the harmonious operation of the entire system and all its proper inhabitants, including the microbes.

WHY BEVERAGES?

Fermented foods take many forms, including solid, liquid, and in between. So what is the special appeal of fermented drinks?

THEY'RE EASY TO INCORPORATE.

First, we may fall into habits more easily around beverages than around solid foods. Many of us have morning routines that include beverages. We also have preferred beverages that we consume with meals or throughout the day. It may be easier to substitute or add fermented beverages into these routines than it would be to substitute or add solid foods.

Drinks can be less challenging than solid foods. Some fermented foods are so pungent they are best used as condiments, in relatively small quantities. Others can be challenging because of their unfamiliar textures. In a few countries, people routinely eat fermented cabbage every day with every meal; but it might be hard to convince the rest of us to eat that much kimchi! A shot of kombucha might be an easier sell in general.

THEY COMPLEMENT MEALS.

Second, it is important to drink the right beverages with our meals. We are frequently told that we must drink lots of water; thus, many of the most health-conscious among us drink lots of water, all the time. But water may not the best thing to drink with meals—especially ice water. There's evidence that too much water can (literally) water down our acidic digestive juices, inhibiting digestion. And cold temperatures generally slow down chemical reactions. Digestion is all about chemical reactions, so we are doing ourselves no favors icing down our digestive tracts while we're eating. Even beyond all of that, drinking too much water at any time of the day can upset the mineral balance in our bodies; in extreme cases, it can lead to death. So naturally fermented beverages are an ideal drink option: They are generally somewhat acidic, and if they're made with the right ingredients, as we will discuss, they contain minerals that our bodies need as well.

THEY'RE APPEALING.

Third, some fermented beverages can be crafted to resemble commercial sodas, making them familiar and appealing to a huge potential audience. Both fermented drinks and sodas can be fizzy, sour, and strongly flavored. The irony of making fermented drinks imitate sodas is this: The fermented drinks existed first, and the commercial ones were originally designed as cheap, easy-to-manufacture imitations of the fermented ones! Some soda names, including root beer and ginger ale, betray this fact. Soda's forced carbonation and potentially toxic phosphoric acid mimic the natural carbonation and healthy lactic acid found in many fermented beverages. And sodas generally incorporate large amounts of industrially produced sugars, which makes them more addictive.

THEY'RE CONVENIENT.

Fourth, beverages are more convenient than solid foods. Beverages are easy to transport and to consume while traveling, even driving. They don't require implements, plates, or napkins; are easier to clean up after; and are easy to portion and to share. And they are easier for the weak, the young, and the elderly to ingest.

THEY'RE QUICK.

Fifth, fermented drinks can be quick to make and/or procure. Some can be prepared in mere minutes. Sometimes, all that's involved is chopping up some vegetables, adding water and sea salt, and waiting. Some excellent fermented beverages and fermented beverage "precursors" are widely available at United States supermarkets: plain yogurt, for example; raw apple cider vinegar; sauerkraut and kimchi; and, increasingly, fermented beverages themselves: kombucha, kvass, kefir, switchel, and others.

THEY'RE GOOD IN COCKTAILS.

And finally, sixth, fermented beverages make great mixed drinks. Cocktails have undergone a renaissance in recent years. Some people want to go beyond the easy, obvious, and classic recipes. Bartenders and amateur mixologists today want to make a name for themselves and are looking for something new and different. See chapter 13 for some ideas for cocktails involving fermented ingredients—it's not a comprehen-

21

FERMENTED CONNECTIONS

Another reason to ferment is for cultural continuity. Passing on our grandmother's recipes and ancestral traditions to our children preserves these links to the past. Understanding the past is important if we want to have a chance at understanding the world around us, a chance at understanding ourselves, and the best possible chance at helping to create a future for coming generations. Deprived of cultures and traditions, we lose some of our humanity.

Yet another reason could best be described as spiritual or energetic. Today, most of us interact all day with digital technology, computers, and remote communications. The electronic revolution has radically and perhaps forever changed the way that we organize, interact, connect, and research. It has also continued the shift that has been taking place in Western culture for centuries: a shift toward the realm of the abstract, toward trusting our heads, and away from trusting our bodies, hearts, and intuitions.

Individuals and families produce less of their own food now than at any other time in history. Reversing this trend by growing food, preparing food, and especially fermenting food and drink is a way for us to engage in a physical rather than abstract way with a realm of life from which we have become estranged and by so doing, reestablish and strengthen our relationships with our own bodies and with our physical aspect. We develop gut feelings, literally, for how plants and foods behave. We discriminate subtleties of taste and smell. We become more attuned to small or large variations in how we feel after incorporating certain foods into ourselves, especially if we have sought those foods with an eye toward improving our health.

When we experience something physically, the physical experience is primary for us, regardless of whether we think we understand the experience intellectually or scientifically. Physical experience can help keep us grounded in the physical world at a time when things around us are getting more and more abstract and virtual. Keeping one foot in the physical world is a choice we can make, and it will benefit us since we are, at least in part, physical beings.

sive guide, but more of a starting point and inspiration for those who want to experiment. And with regards to cocktails, here's something to ponder: Later in the book, we include recipes for fermented coconut water (page 136) and fermented, spiced pineapple wine, known as tepache (page 178). Is it possible that the ancestor of the Piña Colada was actually a sour, refreshing, low-sugar, lightly-alcoholic drink, a drink that you could enjoy all day, rather than the thick, sweet, and strong one that some of us are accustomed to?

22

For newcomers, fermented drinks are an ideal introduction to the world of fermentation. For experienced enthusiasts, new and different beveragescan enliven the fermentation landscape and provide new options. And for everyone, fermented beverages can be fun, delicious, and nutritious.

WHY FERMENT DRINKS YOURSELF?

Depending on where you live, you may already be able to buy a wide variety of fermented beverages, including drinkable yogurts, commercial kefir (which, depending on your local regulations, may be quite different from homemade kefir), kombucha, kvass, fermented coconut water, switchel, and shrub—not to mention raw apple cider vinegar, which isn't drinkable as-is, but can easily be made so. Why would you want to make them yourself?

MICROBIAL DIVERSITY IS ONE REASON. Of necessity, store-bought ferments are made under carefully controlled conditions, often inoculated with a few specific, known microbial strains. You can see this on the side of a carton of yogurt, for example. The best store-bought yogurt contains only two types of ingredients: whole milk and bacterial cultures. Often, the specific cultures are listed, and rarely are there more than three or four. Using specific microbes means that these foods can be produced in large batches with predictable results. Home ferments often contain much larger and more mysterious menageries of microbes than store-bought ferments. The broader slate of microbes can create a greater variety of trace nutrients and may be a better match for our bodies. After all, we're not sure exactly which microbes or nutrients we need in our digestive systems, so the shotgun approach may be more appropriate than a laser approach.

COST IS ANOTHER REASON TO MAKE YOUR OWN FERMENTED BEVERAGES. Store-bought fermented products are almost always more expensive than acquiring raw materials and fermenting at home. This makes sense because of the work involved in making ferments and of the costs of transporting and storing them. The specific economics of home fermentation depend on access to the ingredients. For some people, the price of a quart of good milk at the store may be not too much lower than the price of a quart of good yogurt; if this is the case, it would be almost as cheap to buy the yogurt than to make it. For others, a special circumstance (such as having access to an apple tree) may make an ingredient (apple juice) effectively free or available in great abundance during certain seasons; this may lead them to focus on a particular ferment (fermented apple juice, also known as cider). And some fermented beverages, such as kombucha, can be made with ingredients that are nearly universally available (tea and sugar), and making can be cheaper that buying by a factor of ten!

HUMANS AND MICROBES

In *The Botany of Desire*, Michael Pollan ruminates on the nature of domestication by looking at our relationships with four different plants: the apple, the tulip, cannabis, and the potato. Did we domesticate tulips, for instance, by selecting them, planting them, watering them, and moving them around? Or did they domesticate us, by seducing us so that we would cultivate and multiply them? His conclusion: These stories are really two sides of the same coin. Humans and tulips both benefit from the relationship. His other case studies reveal similar relationships.

The same goes for many other kinds of beings, among them cows, chickens, dogs, and domestic cats. None of these would exist in their present form without us, nor would our lives be the same without them.

There are strains of bacteria, yeast, and mold that can be added to this list. When we ferment food, we cultivate these microbes, thinking about what conditions they need for survival and how to guide them toward our common goal. Even when we are not fermenting food, we are in a relationship with microbes, even if we're not aware of it. We participate in an ongoing exchange of microbes with our environment and with the other humans (and animals and plants) around, via all our surfaces, external and internal, and via the air, the earth, and the water. The microbes in intentionally fermented foods have evolved with humans, and there is a lot of overlap between these microbes and the ones in our guts.

Since the mid-1800s, industrial society has been engaged in a "war on bacteria." The initial sorties were victories for us: Pasteurization gave us greater control over food; and antibiotics enabled us to cure conditions that had been fatal before. A scratch or a small animal bite that might have led to a lost limb or to death before became only a minor event.

We may have taken things too far in this war. We are now killing microbes indiscriminately, with bactericides in soaps, socks, sippy cups, and toothpastes, and we are feeding antibiotics carelessly to humans and to livestock. This is leading to an arms race, humans vs. microbes—

as we deploy new antibiotics, microbes evolve immunity to them. And the way things are going right now, the microbes will get the last laugh. Excessive hygiene weakens our immune systems, which we are discovering are tightly intertwined with our gut bacteria. Excessive hygiene also accelerates the selective evolution of dangerous strains of bacteria, especially in hospitals, where, ironically, the most vulnerable and immunocompromised among us seek refuge. We can't ever kill all the microbes, and we are inadvertently strengthening some of the most dangerous ones.

What was the original goal of the war on bacteria? Improved public health. Somewhere along the way, we lost sight of that goal and became fixated on the fight. Part of the problem is that our relationship with microbes is subtle and not well understood. Western medical science seeks the simplest and most general explanations for phenomena; the broadest theories are often viewed as the most desirable. The preference for simplicity is magnified by our popular press, with its need for 15-second sound bites to match our 15-second attention spans. Often, this means reducing complex phenomena to unrealistically simplistic dichotomies and imperfect analogies. If antibiotics are good, then more antibiotics must be better. If killing some microbes is good, then killing more of them, or all of them, must be better. Unfortunately, it's not that simple.

Capitalism contributes to this trend, too, with the incentives that it creates. When there is market demand for a product, antibiotics for example, and when companies start selling that product, those companies become motivated to create and sell more and more of it. From a business point of view, this is logical, especially when a pharmaceutical compound has been expensive to develop. The more pills that are sold, the easier it is to recoup the initial outlay of money. Companies may not have much choice; their investors demand maximized profits. If company executives do not deliver, their boards will hire new executives, and things will go on as planned. The problem is that maximizing profits may happen without regard for the good of their customers or the public. It is often difficult even to determine what the public good is.

In theory, government and regulatory agencies exist to create balance in these situations. But in practice, approval for new products can be quick, full understanding of long-term effects slow, lobbying dollars powerful, and multinational politics and economics complex and corrupt.

Trying to address these sorts of problems on a large scale may seem daunting. Each of us can start to address them on a small scale, for ourselves, by taking greater charge of our own food and health and rethinking our relationship with microbes. Microbes have made us what we are and vice versa. We rise and fall with them.

25

OUR CULTURED HISTORY

Fermentation has been part of the human experience from the start. We can only guess at some of the earliest events, but it's clear that ferments aren't a recent fad or innovation. Humans have had relationships with fermentation for a long time.

THE DRUNKEN MONKEY

We may have developed our taste for fermented drinks even before we were human.

According to the Drunken Monkey hypothesis, proposed in 2000 by Dr. Robert Dudley in *The Quarterly Review of Biology*, our ancestors were eating fermenting fruit before humans were on the scene. Other animals that weren't ancestors of humans were doing the same. The alcohol and vinegar odor generated by pungent overripe fruit made the fruit easier to find because animals could "follow their nose" to its source. Consuming alcohol in small amounts can increase short-term focus, heighten the senses, and increase appetite, so animals who found some rotting fruit would have been in a better position to find more, thus reinforcing the rotting-fruit-seeking-and-eating behavior. (Studies have demonstrated that consuming alcohol before a meal can increase appetite in modern humans, a phenomenon that has been dubbed "the apértif effect.")

Fruit, fermenting or not, was a useful food source, accessible only to animals who could find it and eat it. These animals got food and calories that other animals did not get, and hence gained some selective reproductive advantage. So this behavior was evolutionarily adaptive, and it spread through populations.

Ten million or so years ago, a genetic mutation drastically increased our ancestors' ability to tolerate alcohol and may have increased their attraction to it. This further increased their advantages over other species, and it helped accelerate some of the changes that differentiate humans from other primates, leaving us with a taste for alcohol.

The Drunken Monkey Hypothesis seems to have gained momentum since it was published in 2000, having been the theme of a symposium and the subject of a book by Dr. Dudley entitled *The Drunken Monkey: Why We Drink and Abuse Alcohol*.

Other researchers and even casual observers have confirmed that we are not the only primates who enjoy fermented drinks. In fact, many inattentive vacationers have had their drinks stolen by aggressive monkeys.

It's hard to assess the accuracy of a theory such as this—our ability to confirm or refute it is limited by our access to events from a very long time ago. Nonetheless, it is an intriguing possibility.

THE STONED APE

Let's also consider Terence McKenna's Stoned Ape theory, as proposed in his 1992 book, *Food of the Gods: The Search for the Original Tree of Knowledge, A Radical History of Plants, Drugs, and Human Evolution*. His theory shares some points with Dudley's, but he looks more deeply into our ancestors' relationships with plants, and he includes more recent history. He observes that hominid evolution moves along at a pace marked by millennia, while by comparison, human culture "presents a spectacle of wild and continuous novelty." He makes a case that our early interactions with plants profoundly affected not only our physical evolution, but also our cultural and linguistic evolution. In his words:

> The early hominids' adoption of an omnivorous diet and their discovery of the power of certain plants were decisive factors in moving early humans out of the stream of animal evolution and into the fast-rising tide of language and culture. Our remote ancestors discovered that certain plants, when self-administered, suppress appetite, diminish pain, supply bursts of sudden energy, confer immunity against pathogens, and synergize cognitive activities. These discoveries set us on the long journey to self-reflection. Once we became tool-using omnivores, evolution itself changed from a process of slow modification of our physical form to a rapid definition of cultural forms by the elaboration of rituals, languages, writing, mnemonic skills, and technology.
>
> These immense changes occurred largely as a result of the synergies between human beings and the various plants with which they interacted and coevolved. An honest appraisal of the impact of plants on the foundations of human institutions would find them to be absolutely primary.

This highlights the importance of plants, fermented plants among them, to humankind.

Twentieth century United States culture was wary of powerful plants—it saw the prohibition of pretty much every popular potent plant-derived preparation, including alcohol. Toward the end of the century in the United States, there was significant growth of interest in good wines and beers. The early twenty-first century sees us decriminalizing cannabis and resuming clinical research into therapeutic uses of psilocybin mushrooms. Home fermentation has grown greatly in popularity in North America. Could this be part of a trend toward a less adversarial stance toward nature?

That is our hope.

FERMENTATION AND CIVILIZATION

For most of human existence, humans were hunter-gatherers or perhaps even scavengers. Early humans would stay around one geographic area as long as it provided them things to hunt, gather, and scavenge; if that location's resources became depleted, they would move on.

In many places, nomadic herders came next. They hunted, they gathered, and they also herded animals. If food and grazing were available, they could stay put, but if food became unavailable, they too would need to decamp.

Twelve thousand or so years ago, some groups started settling for long periods of time in one place, domesticating and cultivating crops. Because we were weren't moving so much and we grew more food than we could eat immediately, we were able, for the first time, to store food for the future. This rise of sedentary agriculture marked the beginning of the Agricultural Revolution and the beginning of what some call "civilization." It led to settlements with higher population density and more permanent living structures. It led to the first stored wealth, in the form of stored food, mostly grain crops. And it led to the first dramatic inequality of wealth and stratification of society because only a few elite people held the keys to the granaries. It also seems to have led to a longer work day and a decline in the general state of health for the non-elites. Part of the decline in health was due to poor nutrition because large parts of the population took up a grain-heavy diet that did not provide the nutrients and variety that the hunter-gatherer diet had; in at least some cases, these newly civilized folk were measurably shorter than their hunter-gatherer forebears, and their skulls showed more signs of under-development, malnourishment, and dental disease. Another part of the health decline was due to the rise of infectious disease, made possible by the increased population density of the new settlements, which accelerated the propagation of new kinds of infectious agents.

Thus characterized, civilization does not sound compelling. Perhaps sedentary agriculture was, as Jared Diamond plainly put it in the title of a 1987 article, "The Worst Mistake in the History of the Human Race." Although it may have been a good thing for the wealthy, agriculture was not an immediate advantage for every-one else.

The advancement of civilization created more work, more crowded conditions, and more sick-ness. (Some people have the same complaints about life today.) So why did we even bother? Why did the civilized way of life win out over hunting and gathering? And there's no doubt

that it has: By the end of the twentieth century, civilization's victory over the hunter-gatherers was nearly complete.

It would be naive to ascribe the rise of civ-ilization to any single factor. And it's worth considering that the most successful societies politically and militarily are not always the most pleasant ones in which to live. Quality of life does not always drive history.

Having said that, one reason these early agri-culturalists might have settled down to grown grain was so that they could make bread. Early sedentary agriculturalists did make bread.

But they also made beer. And in the 1950s in the United States, starting with J.D. Sauer, the Beer Before Bread theory emerged, making the case that beer, not bread, was the primary reason for growing grain. ("Pints over Pastry," quips a 2013 article in *Nautilus* magazine.) In fact, beer has nutritional advantages over bread and is easier to make in some ways, so this idea is not far-fetched. And drinking beer sounds like more fun than eating bread. Perhaps humans settled in cities so that they could have beer!

Thousands of years before the Beer Before Bread theory, the Classical Greek historian and general Thucydides reportedly wrote: "The peo-ples of the Mediterranean began to emerge from barbarism when they learned to cultivate the olive and the vine." The Ancient Greeks were big wine drinkers, not so much beer. But this millennia-old assertion is analogous in some ways to the modern Beer Before Bread theory.

Could it be that fermented beverages domes-ticated humans?

FERMENTATION AND HEALTH

As settlements grew into cities, early urbanites gained some benefit from fermented beverages. For instance, Ancient Greeks and Romans were known to drink their wine mixed with water. Why would you mix wine with water? This may have been driven by practical rather than culinary considerations. First, wine may have been scarce or expensive. Second, it might have been too strong for all-day drinking. But third, and possibly most interestingly, the wine may have been added to the water rather than vice versa.

Wine would have been added to water to treat the water, making it safer to drink. Ancient Greeks and Romans were also known to drink water with vinegar in it, very likely for the same reason—to neutralize some water-borne pathogens. In fact, the line between wine and vinegar might have been more fluid back then. Wild yeast and less hygienic conditions may have led to wine that was more sour to start with. They may not always have been meticulous about keeping their wine in airtight containers all the time, leading to a quicker transition to vinegar. But wine, being valuable, would not have been thrown away even when it became sour. This relationship with wine on its way to vinegar might offer a new perspective on the passages in the New Testament (Matthew and Mark) in which Jesus of Nazareth, while dying, is offered a sponge soaked in vinegar (presumably diluted with water). This sounds like an odd thing to offer someone who is dying, but at the time, it may have made perfect sense. There was even a name for this drink of watered-down vinegar: *posca*.

Beyond their use for sanitizing water, fermented drinks were used as carriers for medicinal plants and herbs. Many plant components are more soluble in alcohol than in water, and alcohol solutions keep better, so many ancient medicines were delivered in an alcohol base. We can see the vestiges of this today in our herbal wines and liqueurs whose origins were medicinal. Vermouth, literally "wormwood," was a wine infused with the wormwood plant, which killed parasites in the intestines.

When it became available, a distilled (strong) alcohol base for herbal potions became popular because stronger alcohol is a more effective solvent. The piquant herbal bouquet of gin reveals its signature herbal ingredient, juniper, which has purported respiratory, hormonal, and digestive benefits. Chartreuse is an herbal liqueur *par excellence* that was originally intended as an elixir for long life and a panacea. It is reported to contain 130 different herbs, plants, and flowers. The exact ingredient list is a closely guarded secret, known to only two living monks at any time.

In the 1980s, while analyzing 1,500-year-old Nubian bones from what is now Sudan, scientist George Armelagos made a startling discovery. These bones showed evidence of exposure to large doses of modern antibiotics. Eventually, Armelagos and chemist Mark Nelson co-authored a paper in which they concluded that this Nubian population had been intentionally brewing beer

31

made with a *Streptomyces* microbe that produced tetracycline. Tetracycline is a modern
antibiotic—it is so important today that it is on
the World Health Organization's *Model List
of Essential Medicines*. Armelagos describes
how surprising this discovery was: "If you were
unwrapping an Egyptian mummy and suddenly
it had Ray-Ban sunglasses on it, that's what it
was like with us." And these brewers from 500
CE seem to have been making it intentionally.

When antibiotics were rediscovered in the
first half of the twentieth century, they were
also by-products of fermentation, in this case
produced by the *Penicillium notatum* mold. So
in modern times as in the past, microbes and
fermentation play an important role in medicine
and public health.

32

FERMENTATION
AND RELIGION

Fermented drinks are so important to religion that even during prohibition in the United States, Americans could legally drink wine in ceremonial contexts. In fact, fermented drinks have played central roles in religion and ritual from Ancient Greece to modern times. Here are a few examples.

The *libation* is a ritual in which some amount of a drink, usually alcoholic, is poured on the ground. Depending on where and when it takes place, the libation might be an offering to a deity, a spirit, or the earth herself. In Ancient Greece and Rome, the gods of wine (Dionysus or Bacchus, respectively) and other gods would receive this observance once a day and more frequently on important occasions. Throughout history, it has parallels in cultures in Africa, Asia and South Asia, and the Americas. Today, libations in different cultures are offered variously for the Saints, for the Devil, and for "my homies" (i.e., friends, in this case, generally deceased).

Wine plays an important role in the spiritual tradition of Judaism as well. There is a ritual prayer over wine at the beginning of the Sabbath every week, and it is used to usher in most holidays. A proper Passover seder involves drinking four glasses of wine in one night—before the meal even starts!

The Eucharist, or the Holy Communion, is an important rite in many Christian churches. In this rite, a reenactment of the Last Supper, bread and wine are sanctified, meaning they become the body and the blood of Christ or become associated with it. The bread may be unleavened (unfermented), as would have been the case at the Last Supper. Or by contrast, in Eastern churches, fermented leavened bread is used for communion, with the yeast in the bread symbolizing the Holy Spirit!

Before the Spanish conquest in what is now Mexico's central highlands, the maguey plant played a crucial role in the life of the Aztecs. As the Greeks and Romans had for wine, the Aztecs had a deity for maguey—the goddess Mayahuel. Pulque, the fermented sap of the maguey, was normally reserved for the royal family, for priests, for retirees, and for those being put to death. Everyone else could have it only occasionally during religious ceremonies.

A more modern commentator on religion, Benjamin Franklin, wrote in a letter to l'abbé André Morellet, probably in 1779: "*Voilà l'eau qui tombe des cieux sur nos vignobles; là, elle entre les racines des vignes pour être changée en vin; preuve constante que Dieu nous aime, et qu'il aime à nous voir heureux.*" That is, "See there the rain that falls from the skies upon our vineyards; there, it enters the roots of the vines to be changed into wine; constant evidence that God loves us, and that God loves to see us happy."

FERMENTATION, SCIENCE, AND HEALTH

You can make fermented drinks without an advanced degree in biochemistry or microbiology. After all, humans fermented nicely for thousands or tens of thousands of years before anyone had heard of microbes.

Biochemistry is not the only model for how fermentation works. Different cultures have different models that may be just as helpful, or may be more helpful, even if these models might not be as "scientific" or as broadly applicable or generalizable to other phenomena.

For instance, some cultures believe that the vessels they have used to ferment are sacred. When using a new vessel for the first time, they will place it among some veteran vessels so the old ones can "teach" the new one. This tactic works equally well whether you believe that the agent of fermentation is a spirit or a microbe.

Nonetheless, it can be helpful to have a mental model for what's going on when you ferment. Having a model is particularly helpful when things don't go the way you hoped they would, so you have some idea of what sorts of changes might result in a better outcome. A little bit of understanding can go a long way.

The study of biochemistry provides one such model.

CRASH COURSE
IN BIOCHEMISTRY

Atoms are individual chemical building blocks of matter. We know of more than 100 different types of atoms, called elements; you've probably heard of many of them, including hydrogen, oxygen, carbon, and nitrogen. For this discussion, let's assume that all atoms of the same element are interchangeable and behave identically. (This is not quite true, but close enough for our purposes.) We'll also assume that atoms of one element can't change into the atoms of another. (This is also not quite true.)

Molecules are clumps of atoms joined in specific three-dimensional arrangements. If two molecules consist of the same atoms stuck together in the same arrangement, they are said to be the same chemical compound. Some examples of compounds are water (two hydrogen atoms and one oxygen, H_2O), carbon dioxide (CO_2), oxygen gas (O_2), table sugar (sucrose, $C_{12}H_{22}O_{11}$), drinking alcohol (ethanol, C_2H_6O), and acetic acid (the acid in vinegar, $C_2H_4O_2$).

The same collection of atoms can sometimes be stuck together in a different way to produce a different compound. For instance, glucose (also known as dextrose), fructose, and galactose all have the same chemical formula, or ingredient list—$C_6H_{12}O_6$—but within the molecules of each of these compounds, the atoms are arranged differently. We call compounds with identical formulas isomers. (*Isomer* means "equal parts"

36

in Greek.) Isomers may exhibit different chemical and physical properties because of their different spatial geometries.

When a collection of atoms or molecules combines and/or splits, resulting in a different collection, this is called a chemical reaction. An example of a chemical reaction is when ethyl alcohol (ethanol) and oxygen gas combine, resulting in acetic acid (also known as ethanoic acid and the key component in vinegar) and

37

ELEMENTS OF ALCHEMY

For a long time, mainstream scientists thought that elements were immutable. Renegades known as alchemists thought otherwise and spent their time trying to transmute one element into another. The alchemists were mocked for their belief. But it turns out that they were right, although it was not until the discovery of nuclear reactions that we understood how it was possible to transmute elements.

water. This is the reaction that makes your wine turn sour when it's exposed to air. It can be represented as follows:

$$C_2H_6O + O_2 \rightarrow C_2H_4O_2 + H_2O$$
$$\text{ethanol} + \text{oxygen} \rightarrow$$
$$\text{ethanoic (acetic) acid plus water}$$

(As the chemists in the audience are aware, this characterization is a significant oversimplification of the situation.)

If you count the total number of atoms of each element on the left and right sides of the arrow, you'll see that they're the same. This is true of any chemical reaction (although as noted before, it is not true of nuclear, or alchemical, reactions). Sometimes, heat is increased by the reaction. This is called an *exothermic* reaction. If heat is consumed, then it is an *endothermic* reaction.

Metabolism is the sum total of all the chemical reactions that happen inside an organism to keep it alive, including reactions that release energy for the organism's use, reactions that create physical building blocks, reactions that play roles in other processes of the organism's body, and more. Metabolism is interesting to us for a few reasons. First, without metabolism there would be no life. But also, the metabolic processes of microbes produce, as by-products, the acids, alcohols, flavors, and bubbles that constitute fermented drinks.

Proteins are large molecules with complex shapes that can fit together like puzzle pieces, or like keys in locks, with other molecules. When they join like this, interesting things can happen. This general mechanism underlies most life processes.

Enzymes, for our purposes, are proteins that catalyze particular biochemical reactions—their presence enables reactions to happen under circumstances where they would not have otherwise, or enables them to happen quicker than they would have otherwise. All living organisms produce enzymes in order to accelerate and favor certain chemical metabolic reactions. For example, digestive enzymes play an important role in digestion.

Carbohydrates are molecules containing

38

carbon, hydrogen, and oxygen in certain proportions and arrangements. Sugars, starches, and fibers are all varieties of carbohydrate. When larger carbohydrates break down, often with the help of enzymes, they become smaller carbohydrates, and ultimately, they become simple sugars.

Simple sugars, or *monosaccharides*, are the smallest carbohydrates. The key monosaccharides in fermentation are glucose, fructose, and galactose—all isomers of $C_6H_{12}O_6$. Glucose, also known as dextrose, is the simple sugar most easily metabolized; fructose is a simple sugar found in many fruits that can be converted by the body into glucose; and finally, galactose is a component in milk sugar and can also be converted into glucose.

Disaccharides are carbohydrates consisting of two simple sugars. The most important disaccharides are sucrose, lactose, and maltose. Roughly speaking, sucrose is a glucose plus a fructose; lactose is a glucose plus a galactose; and maltose is two glucoses.

Oligosaccharides are carbohydrates consisting of at least two but no more than ten-ish simple sugars. *Polysaccharides* are carbohydrates consisting of two or three or more simple sugars. *Complex carbohydrates* are carbohydrates consisting of many simple sugars (there's no specific number).

Microbes are microscopic living organisms. Although the individual organisms are microscopic, colonies of them can sometimes become visible to the human eye. The key microbes for fermentation are bacteria, yeasts, and molds.

Bacteria are single-celled organisms and some of the oldest forms of life on the earth, dating back at least 3.5 billion years.

Yeasts are more complicated single-celled organisms that have been around for hundreds of millions of years.

Molds are biologically similar to yeasts in some ways, but grow in multicellular agglomerations.

What does all of this scientific theory have to do with fermented drinks?

Some bacteria and yeasts can *cleave* disaccharides and to a lesser extent bigger polysaccharides into simple sugars. Then they can convert the simple sugars into acids, alcohol, and gasses.

That's what gets us fermented drinks—sour, fizzy, and sometimes alcoholic.

A simple lactic acid reaction looks like this:

$$C_6H_{12}O_6 \rightarrow 2 \times C_3H_6O_3$$
glucose $\rightarrow$ 2 molecules of lactic acid

A more complicated one looks like this:

$$C_6H_{12}O_6 \rightarrow C_3H_6O_3 + C_2H_6O + CO_2$$
glucose $\rightarrow$ lactic acid + ethanol + carbon dioxide

Acid, alcohol, and bubbles—now we're talking!

Some bacteria convert ethyl alcohol into acetic acid, via a reaction we saw earlier:

$$C_2H_6O + O_2 \rightarrow C_2H_4O_2 + H_2O$$
ethanol + oxygen $\rightarrow$
acetic (ethanoic) acid plus water

FERMENTING WITH MOLD

Molds are key to some kinds of fermented drinks—rice ferments such as amazake, traditional soju and shōchū, and sake. These drinks were not included in this book because they are harder to make, and they may not coexist happily in proximity to other ferments— that is, they involve more work, require more temperature control, and are sensitive to cross-contamination from bacterial ferments.

Sake may be the king of mold-fermented drinks. It is not a project to be undertaken lightly—making sake can take the better part of a year! And there are other important fermented foods involving molds. Notable examples include many sorts of cheeses (such as blue cheeses and bloomy-rind cheeses); dried sausages; traditionally-brewed soy sauce; and miso.

A reaction whereby yeasts convert glucose or fructose into alcohol looks like this:

$$C_6H_{12}O_6 \rightarrow 2 \times C_2H_6O + 2 \times CO_2$$

glucose or fructose →

2 molecules of ethanol

+ 2 molecules of carbon dioxide

This yeast reaction is key to almost all alcoholic drinks, as well as (leavened) bread.

Again, these are huge simplifications, and these are by no means the only reactions that take place, but they do give us a mental picture of what's happening.

When we are fermenting a drink, all the sugars and starches (carbohydrates) in the starting formula generally do one of four things: they remain carbohydrates; they become alcohols; they become acids; and/or some small amount may evaporate. "Serious" brewers take advantage of this equation, estimating alcohol levels indirectly by measuring or interpolating the density and sugar level of their liquid at different stages in the brewing process.

How much sugar gets converted into what depends on a variety of factors, but the general trend is from sugar to alcohol to acid. Understanding and internalizing this concept can help us adjust our formulas and processes. For instance, if you're making Tepache (a pineapple wine—see page 178) and you'd like it to have more alcohol, you might need to add more sugar and let it ferment for longer, or you might need to restrict access to oxygen sooner to slow down the conversion to acid. Or if you'd like it to be less sour, you could try fermenting it for a shorter period (although tepache will always be pretty sour!) and/or restricting access to oxygen. Finally, if your drink fermenting experiment fails, you may still be able to get a nice vinegar out of it, just by giving it full access to oxygen and letting it ferment until all the sugar and all the alcohol have become acid.

WHAT IS HEALTH?

Health is a surprisingly subtle concept.

It's most simply defined as "the state of being free from illness or injury." This is a start, but it's inadequate. It talks about what health isn't, not directly about what health is. It's quite abstract and even possibly circular: What is illness if not "the absence of health?"

The World Health Organization goes further, saying that "[health] is a state of complete physical, mental, and social well-being and not merely the absence of disease or infirmity." This gives us a bit more to hold on to. If health is not merely the absence of disease and infirmity, maybe it's the opposite of disease and infirmity—ease and robustness? Ease and robustness seem to be good indicators of health.

But even this last definition leaves something to be desired. It sounds absolute and unachievable.

We might do better to think of health as a spectrum and to think of it as being assessed with a particular context in mind. Life forms can exist in varying degrees of health. Furthermore, a state of being that might be optimal in one context might not be optimal in another. Perhaps we can think of health as a measure of the degree to which your body, mind, and spirit are suited to the context in which you live, allowing you to go about your business with ease and robustness.

Optimal health for a hunter-gatherer could be different from optimal health for a chef or an office worker. You could argue that humans evolved to be hunter-gatherers and not desk-sitters, and so health should be measured by our hunter-gatherer fitness; but the majority of humans, including most of those reading this book, are not hunter-gatherers. So, the point seems moot.

Let's focus on the idea of improving health, or optimizing health, for one individual human (and necessarily for her or his concomitant ecosystem of microbes!) in that human's context. An improvement of health is a change that makes life easier and increases resilience.

Different people face different health challenges. Some of us would like to lose weight, and some of us urgently *need* to lose weight. Excess weight is often a result of a metabolic issue, a digestive one, and/or a behavioral or psychological one. Excess weight correlates with type 2 diabetes. Others of us have challenges that present explicitly digestive symptoms—acid reflux, gas and bloating, and problems with elimination. (Think back to the "opioid-induced constipation" from chapter 1; in this case, the pathogenesis is clear.)

Problems typically seen as nutritional deficiencies can often be traced to problems of incomplete digestion. A propensity toward frailness and catching colds and flu or flu-like maladies points toward a weak immune system, which is being increasingly understood as linked to gut microbiology. Long-term aches and pains or allergies may indicate autoimmune problems, which means (give or take) that your

41

immune system is "confused" about something that's going on in your body—this too may have its root and may find its resolution in the gut.

Finally, some inscrutable, difficult-to-treat conditions, Parkinson's and autism for instance, seem to correlate with changes in gut physiology. Mainstream medicine is just starting to explore these gut connections. Alternative medicine practitioners have been a decade or two (or perhaps a few centuries!) ahead on noticing these connections. If you're interested, check out the book *Gut and Psychology Syndrome* by Dr. Natasha Campbell-McBride.

A good many of today's biggest health problems seem to be gut-related, even if they do not immediately seem like digestive problems.

Furthermore, different people's bodies react differently to changes in diet and behavior. This is a facet of a concept known as *bio-individuality*: we are all the same species, and our genetics are very similar, but our bodies work differently, and what helps one person may hurt another.

So when discussing the health benefits of fermented foods for *you*, it's important to keep in mind what your health goals are. Do you have specific issues you're trying to address? Or do you feel good about your health, and you want to do everything you can to maintain it?

Read this section of the book with an eye toward your own specific goals, and it may help you focus your energy to help achieve them!

HEALTH BENEFITS

We've started hearing more and more about the health benefits of fermented foods and drinks. It's no longer a fringe topic—today even the mainstream media are addressing it.

But the mainstream media are often not able to spend sufficient time on subtle subjects such as this one, and they often do not provide enough context for meaningful discussions about public health. On top of that, the media are overly eager to quantify things, assigning unrealistically precise numbers and percentages so that they can sound more "scientific" in cases where these numbers are not terribly meaningful. For instance, even if a scientific study calculates a percentage reduction in the rate of some disease that is correlated with some diet or lifestyle change, that percentage may be only vaguely relevant to any given individual, and other factors may be much more important than that particular change.

That said, what are the health benefits of fermented drinks, and what's the best way to discuss them? More specifically: How could consuming this fermented drink affect my health, compared with drinking nothing at all? Another related question might be: How could this fermented drink affect my health, compared with unfermented alternatives? Some alternatives might include raw drinks, pasteurized or ultra-pasteurized drinks, sugary industrial sodas, sports drinks, distilled alcohol drinks, and water.

Here are some of the ways in which fermented drinks can help support our health. Not all the benefits are fully understood, and not every fermented drink provides every benefit—which is a good reason to consume as wide a variety of fermented drinks as is practical for you, wherever you are on your fermented drink journey.

FERMENTED DRINKS CONTAIN LIVE, "FRIENDLY" MICROBES.

Furthermore, they don't contain pathogenic, "bad" ones. Exclusion of bad microbes is one of the key advantages of fermented drinks over water and fresh drinks. Without bad microbes, a drink is safer and less likely to make us sick.

Friendly microbes are similar or identical to some of the microbes that are necessary for a healthy human gut. (This is not a coincidence—these microbes have evolved alongside, and inside, us.) Most of the microbes that we ingest do not survive the long journey through our digestive system; there's some debate about exactly how many do survive, but it's very likely that some of them do, judging from the kinds of health changes that people report when they start consuming fermented products.

Taking probiotic supplement pills is another way to ingest microbes. These pills are generally coated to ensure the survival of many of the microbes into our gut. But these supplements do not necessarily contain the wide *variety* of microbes that a home ferment contains. And if they're not transported and stored carefully, probiotic supplements can die. (By contrast, bubbly fermented drinks are pretty clearly alive.)

When we ingest microbes, by whatever means, some of them join and interact with the microbes already in our bodies, strengthening our own biological processes such as digestion and immune function. In addition, given their short lifecycle, it's possible that the microbes in our gut literally evolve in response to their environment; so even if we don't ingest the microbes we need, they might become the microbes we're looking for somewhere down the road.

A healthy gut flora can help us maintain or even restore the lining of our gut. This improves our body's resistance to bad microbes that might lead to symptoms of food poisoning; it decreases the degree to which inorganic toxins (heavy metals for instance) are absorbed into our body; it decreases the tendency for partially-digested proteins to pass into our blood, provoking undesirable immune responses; and it may help us in other ways that we do not yet understand.

UNFILTERED FERMENTED DRINKS OFTEN CONTAIN YEAST.

Yeast, alive or dead, is a source of various B vitamins and can be a source of small amounts of protein and of some important trace minerals such as selenium and chromium. Fermented drinks can also contain other important nutrients, including A and C vitamins, K vitamins, enzymes, and antioxidants of various sorts that we are only starting to understand (polyphenols, flavonoids, resveratrol, etc.).

MANY VITAMINS AND ALL ENZYMES ARE DESTROYED BY EXPOSURE TO HEAT.

This denaturing happens progressively between approximately 118°F and 180°F (48°C and 82°C). Fermenting without heat leaves vitamins and enzymes intact. This differentiates fermented drinks from, say, unfermented store-bought fruit juice, almost all of which is pasteurized.

FERMENTED DRINKS CONTAIN ACIDS, ALCOHOLS, OR (USUALLY) A BIT OF BOTH.

Both have the potential to keep pathogenic microbes at bay, staving off digestive problems, and increasing the lifespan of food. And for most people, consumption of small to moderate amounts of alcohol can provide benefits to the cardiovascular system, to the nervous system (including brain function), and to the liver. It can increase libido and appetite for food. Of course, too much alcohol can cause problems. The dose makes the poison, as the Swiss-German philosopher Paracelsus observed in the 1500s. This is a case in which we must rein in our desire to see the world in simple, good-vs.-bad terms.

FERMENTED DRINKS CAN BE MORE DIGESTIBLE THAN THEIR RAW COUNTERPARTS.

Certain foods contain starches that are difficult to digest. For example, eating a lot of raw cabbage can lead to gas. But fermented cabbage contains fewer of these tricky starches—microbes have predigested some of them. So eating sauerkraut or kimchi, or drinking juiced kraut or kimchi, can give you the benefits of the cabbage, plus the benefits of fermentation, without the digestive challenges.

FERMENTATION CAN INCREASE THE BIOAVAILABILITY OF NUTRIENTS THAT OCCUR NATURALLY IN FOODS.

Phytic acid, for instance, is a compound that occurs in foods and drinks. It binds certain minerals in a way that causes them to pass through the body undigested. Fermentation can break down phytic acid, providing us access to minerals that otherwise would have been lost.

FERMENTED DRINKS DON'T USE INDUSTRIAL PRESERVATIVES AND METHODS.

Industrial chemical preservatives and physical processes are good at preserving food. Unfortunately, some of them are discovered to be toxic, maybe carcinogenic, sometimes many years after they are introduced. Neither food regulators nor industrial producers want to arrange and perform the 20- or 30-year experiments that would be necessary to figure these things out before market releases. The experiment is done on the public. The choice is yours: Would you like to be part of the experiment group and ingest these new things, many never seen before by the human body? Or would you like to be part of the control group and not ingest them?

FERMENTED DRINKS VERSUS OTHER DRINKS

How does the competition stack up?

- **WATER:** Compared with water, fermented drinks contain more minerals, more vitamins, and sometimes more protein. Microbiologically, they're safer because of the acids, the alcohols, and the microbes that they contain.

- **RAW FRUIT JUICE:** Compared with raw fruit juice, fermented drinks contain more probiotic microbes, more nutrients, and more beneficial acids. They can also contain significantly less sugar. And fermented drinks are safer to drink, have a significantly longer shelf life, and are more digestible. They may also contain some alcohol.

- **CANNED FRUIT JUICE:** Canned and boxed juices are heat-treated, so they lose the enzymes and some of the vitamins that fresh juices may have, and some of them contain industrial preservatives as well. Sometimes synthetic vitamins are added back in, but only the ones that we know about and sometimes in forms that may not be as bioavailable. The only advantage that canned juices have over fresh ones is their shelf life. Fermented drinks win again. And in fact, fermenting can be an excellent way of remedying the "deadness" of the canned and boxed juices, imparting enzymes, vitamins, and live microbes to them.

- **MILK:** Ultra-pasteurized milk is similar in many ways to canned or boxed juice. It is shelf-stable and dead. It used to be sold in rectangular boxes, but when the public in the United States rejected these boxes, dairy distributors put the boxed milk back into familiar cartons and put it back in the refrigerated section; this illusion of perishability helps sales. Pasteurized milk is a little better than ultra-pasteurized milk, but not much. Fermenting either of these milks into kefir or yogurt can give it new life. (Some people report difficulties fermenting ultra-pasteurized milk; others encounter no problems.)

- **SODA:** Industrial sodas generally contain no nutrients or enzymes whatsoever; have a lot of sugar, often in forms that lead to weight gain and diabetes; and have potentially problematic ingredients, such as phosphoric acid and large amounts of caffeine. Natural fermented sodas are better than industrial sodas in every way.

- **SPORTS DRINKS:** So-called sports drinks are mostly water, with the addition of spiffy coloring, refined salt, high fructose corn syrup, artificial sweeteners and flavorings, some oil or glycol to impart mouthfeel, and some sort of acid to make them taste less sweet. Compare this with salty lemonade, made with salty preserved (fermented) lemons and some sugar. Or compare with a pint (500 ml) of water with a tablespoon (15 g) of sugar and a pinch of sea salt; in this case, the primary benefit may not come from the fermentation, but simply from not drinking the sports drink. You're better off replacing it with almost anything with a pinch of salt and bit of natural sugar!

- **COFFEE AND TEA:** Coffee and tea have many interesting qualities, potential benefits, and potential challenges—too many to discuss here. Fortunately, sweetened tea and coffee are fermentable, quite deliciously (see Kombucha, page 105).

45

BEFORE YOU START

The recipes in this book share many tools, concepts, and ingredients, some of which are described here. Before you start shopping, keep in mind that you don't need every tool for every recipe. In fact, if you are a devout minimalist, you can get by with nothing more than a tablespoon measure and a few Mason jars. This chapter will help you think about the tools you already have, how you can use them, what you may want or need, and what you may not need.

MEASURING TOOLS

People in different parts of the world use different systems of measurement. In the United States, we mostly use U.S. customary units, which include teaspoons, tablespoons, ounces, cups, pints, quarts, and gallons. Much of the rest of the world use the metric system, which includes grams for weight, liters for volume, and fractions and multiples of grams and liters.

The U.S. system distinguishes *liquid* volume measurement and *dry* volume measurement, while the metric system does not. Confusingly, the U.S. system uses the same words for liquid and dry measures, but they are not exactly equal. For instance, a U.S. liquid quart is 0.946 (metric) liters, whereas a U.S. dry quart is 1.101 liters. Most U.S. cookbooks blur or do not make this distinction.

Then there's weight to consider. A liquid quart is exactly 32 fluid ounces (by volume). A quart of liquid may weigh more or less than 32 ounces (by weight): 32 fluid ounces of water weighs a little more than 32 ounces, but some liquids, such as honey, are denser than water—32 fluid ounces of honey might weigh 50 ounces, for example. And temperature is another factor that affects the weight of water and other liquids.

To further illustrate this variation, consider the saying, "The pint's a pound, the world around." As you may suspect by now, it's not that simple. We can qualify the saying a bit by saying that a U.S. pint of water weighs close to a pound (16 ounces), depending on temperature and perhaps other factors. (And in general, the weight of a pint of your favorite fermented beverage will be within 10% of the weight of a pint of water, and likely much closer.) But a U.K. pint is 20% bigger than a U.S. pint, so a U.K. pint of water weighs about 20 ounces, which is definitely different from a pound. And Canada and Australia officially define a cup to be a quarter of a liter, so in those countries, you may get a "pint" of beer that turns out to be a half-liter, which is approximately 16.9 fluid ounces, somewhere between a U.S. pint and a U.K. pint.

The good news is that drink fermenting is tolerant of minor variations such as these. So to keep things as simple as possible, in this book, we'll use the following imprecise equivalences between U.S. and metric (see page 50). (Do not assume that you can use these conversions for recipes that you find anywhere else!)

2 POUNDS ≈
1 KILOGRAM

1 QUART ≈
1 LITER

1 OUNCE ≈
30 GRAMS ≈
30 MILLILITERS

1 TABLESPOON ≈
15 GRAMS ≈
15 MILLILITERS

1 TEASPOON ≈
5 GRAMS ≈
5 MILLILITERS

If you use all U.S. measures or if you use all metric measures, the ratios of ingredients in the recipes will be very close to what is intended. If you mix and match U.S. and metric (a quart of water with 90 grams of sugar, or a liter of water with 3 ounces of sugar), you might get some variation, but the recipes should still work.

That said, if you can, your best bet is to get a small electronic kitchen scale and measure weights using grams. These scales are available inexpensively in stores or via the Internet. And you may find yourself using the scale, and the metric system, for other recipes, too! In particular, the best baking cookbooks all specify ingredients in grams and kilograms because precision is important in baking.

Mason jars are available in both U.S. and metric sizes. Again, for our purposes, the 5% difference between a quart and a liter can be ignored.

JAR EQUIPMENT

YOU MAY WANT THE FOLLOWING:

- Mason jars and lids
- A canning funnel (stainless steel or plastic)
- A nylon mesh strainer that fits in the top of the canning funnel
- Chlorine-free, basket-style paper coffee filters, or clean handkerchiefs, or paper towels
- A wide mouth lid with a built-in airlock

Mason jars are inexpensive, durable glass jars originally intended for high-temperature canning and food storage. They have seen wide use in a variety of applications and are particularly well suited to fermenting. They are sold under various brand names, including Ball, Kerr, and Bernardin, in two common mouth sizes: standard mouth (70 mm outer diameter) and wide mouth (86 mm). They are generally sold with two-part metal canning lids. The jars themselves are dishwasher safe; the lids will start to corrode if you put them in the dishwasher because of the abrasiveness and alkalinity of dishwashing powder, so they are best washed by hand. You can often find jars secondhand or at yard sales, for instance.

GASES AND AIRLOCKS

When you ferment things, you often generate gases in the process. Some of the gases dissolve in the food or drink you're fermenting, making it fizzy. But if you are fermenting in a Mason jar with a closed lid, you'll need to manage these gases.

If you find yourself in this situation, it's possible to leave a Mason jar lid a little loose, allowing the gasses to escape. It's also okay to tighten the lid fully and then "burp" it periodically by opening it briefly until it stops hissing and then closing it. If you forget or miscalculate, it's usually not disastrous—the jars themselves are stronger than the lids, so excess gas will (generally!) bend the lid and escape rather than breaking the glass jar. Still, it's better to avoid destroying too many lids.

Another option is to buy lids with actual airlocks built in. Airlocks are one-way valves that allow gases to escape without letting outside air in, so you won't have to relieve the pressure in your jars manually. Recently, a variety of different airlock designs have become available. The ones that use water traps have been used successfully by fermenters for years, but for convenience, you might prefer the ones without water traps, since airlock water can sometimes evaporate or get contaminated or messy.

Mason jars are quite versatile. Some have measures on their sides and can be used as measuring cups in applications that don't require great precision (e.g. fermenting). They can also be used as drinking glasses (smaller ones for smaller drinks and bigger ones for big drinks!).

And in recent years, many Mason jar accoutrements have appeared on the market. A variety of lids are available: plastic lids that can be put in the dishwasher; plastic and silicone sippy-cup lids and lids with holes for straws; lids with a variety of different kinds of integrated airlocks, specifically intended for fermenting; lids to help you sprout grains; decorative lids, intended for holding flowers and such; cocktail strainer lids; and so on. There are also Mason jar holders and cozies that provide insulation for hot and cold beverages. There are even kits to convert Mason jars into French press coffee makers, lamps, nightlights, salt and pepper shakers, Bluetooth speakers, and more.

The following are some of the most popular sizes:

- 8-ounce (cup, or 250 ml) standard mouth
- 16-ounce (pint, 500 ml) wide mouth
- 32-ounce (quart, or 1 liter) wide mouth
- 64-ounce (half gallon, or 2 liter) wide mouth

There are two less common in-between sizes that deserve mention: 12-ounce standard mouth and 24-ounce wide mouth. The 12-ounce (375 ml) jar is a good one for drinking a modest portion of your favorite fermented drink. The 24-ounce (750 ml) wide mouth jar is the largest standard size that has straight sides, making it easy to clean, easy to store, and great for storing frozen liquids—the lack of a shoulder makes it easier to get icebergs out. (If you are freezing it, be sure to leave the lid nice and loose—otherwise you risk broken jars!)

A canning funnel is a wide funnel with a broad "tip" that fits into the top of Mason jars. It's useful for getting splashy or chunky things into Mason jars without making a mess. The funnel can also hold a good-size strainer. Canning funnels and strainers come into play in some of the recipes here. They're useful around the kitchen for other things too.

Some recipes call for having ferments breathe while they're fermenting. Leaving jars completely uncovered is not recommended; animals, dirt, and other foreign objects will soon find their way in. The best option is to use a permeable paper or cloth cover, secured with the ring portion of the Mason jar lid or with a rubber band. Coffee filters, clean cloth handkerchiefs, and paper towels all work well. Cheesecloth is not as good—if it is too coarse, it can let bugs through! Flies and vinegar eels are not life-threatening problems, but they generally mean throwing away your ferment, washing everything thoroughly, and starting over again.

If you love Mason jars and you have a lot of them, you can use them for just about everything, and you don't truly *need* any other jars or bottles or much other equipment at all. But other kinds of vessels are better or easier for some things.

WHICH LID, AND WHEN?

Generally, if you are trying to build up alcohol, you'll want to ferment with a closed lid or an airlock; if you are aiming for carbonation, you'll want a closed lid; but if you are aiming for a sour fermentation, then breathing is probably best.

Fermentation airlocks for bottles and jars.

STORAGE BOTTLES AND JARS

YOU MAY WANT THE FOLLOWING:

- Glass jugs of various sizes (also known as carboys, growlers, or demijohns)

- Airlocks, stoppers, and lids for the jugs

- Flip-top (also known as swing-top or Grolsch-style) bottles in various sizes, and/or wine bottles with corks

Some ferments prefer less exposure to air. These are best brewed in small-mouthed vessels. Large glass jugs, or carboys, are good candidates. These are available in a variety of sizes, including very large ones, allowing you to make very large batches if you wish. In the United States, apple juice is often sold in gallon (4 L) glass jugs, which work great for making gallon-sized batches of hard apple cider—you get the ingredient and the equipment in one shot! Beer and sometimes kombucha are sold in half gallon (2 L) growlers from local breweries. Keep the bottle and don't forget to keep the cap too. If you would like a jug larger than a gallon, check a local homebrew shop or the Internet. Larger jugs can be significantly more expensive than gallon jugs of apple juice, but you probably won't need many larger jugs.

Glass is the best material for jugs. Plastic jugs are cheaper, lighter, and easier to find, but the plastic could potentially leach from the jug into your drink. Some plastic containers are classified as food-safe by various authorities and agencies. Food-safe does not mean that they don't leach—it just means that leaching is limited to a certain amount, which is a function of surface area, liquid acidity levels, duration of storage, and so on. A fermenting jug has a lot of surface area, and you may be leaving your drink in it for quite a while. If part of your reason for fermenting is to improve your health, then you probably want to limit your intake of plastic. You may already be getting plastic in other foods that you're eating, especially if you eat in restaurants a lot or if you use a microwave. You can choose your battles and decide whether the convenience of a plastic carboy outweighs the risk. It's hard to really know. Some folks will conclude that it's best to play it safe.

Once you have your jugs, you will also want some airlocks with stoppers, especially if you are not able to tend your ferments daily (to burp them). Homebrew shops are a good place to find these airlocks, or you can buy them online.

One of the fun things about fermented beverages is their fizziness. The problem is that you can lose a lot of fizz when you pour your drinks from large brewing vessels into portion-size bottles or jars. Fortunately, there are ways to limit this fizz loss. A siphon pump and/or a suitable length of flexible hosing and some improvisation

55

can allow you to get the liquid out of jugs with a minimal loss of bubbles. Siphon pumps are plastic, but because of the short duration of contact with your drinks, they don't raise the same concerns as plastic brewing jugs.

The process of moving your ferment out of the carboy or kombucha jar into smaller bottles is called (not surprisingly) bottling. You don't absolutely have to bottle your drinks, but doing so lets you keep more of the fizz, lets you move them into the refrigerator for storage, and makes it possible to perform secondary fermentation in the bottle (see page 112). Many sorts of bottles can be used for bottling. If you are ambitious, you can use beer bottles and get a bottle-capping machine, but this is not at all necessary.

In fact, Mason jars are fine, and if you bottle in the same jars you're going to serve in, you eliminate one round of pouring, decrease waste, and simplify cleanup. Flip-top Grolsch-style bottles are nice too, and because of their narrow neck, they preserve fizz for longer once they're open; they are also fancier-looking than Mason jars. Empty bottles from store-bought kombucha are a great choice, too, because they are designed to be strong enough to hold a carbonated drink. Even wine bottles with corks will do for some ferments, although they can't hold fizz as well as the others, and they're not as durable.

KOMBUCHA SUPPLIES

YOU MAY WANT THE FOLLOWING:

- A one- or two-gallon (4 L or 8 L), cylindrical glass cookie jar–style container, with or without a built-in spigot near the bottom; or a small wooden barrel

- A large handkerchief, kitchen towel, or unbleached basket-type coffee filter that can cover the top of the cookie jar, plus a rubber band or string to secure it

- A siphon pump (optional)

Because of the microbes involved, kombucha needs to breathe while it's brewing. An ideal brewing vessel is a 2-gallon (8 L) glass cookie jar–style container approximately as wide as it is tall. A similarly-dimensioned wooden barrel, open on one end (the top), is another possibility. If these are too heavy for you to lift, you can use smaller containers. They're all likely to work better than a Mason jar, for a few reasons. First, Mason jars larger than a half gallon (2 L) are hard to find, and a half gallon (2 L) batch is on the small side if you like drinking kombucha. Additionally, when brewing kombucha, the ratio of jar width to height plays a factor in maintaining the balance between the bacteria and the yeast. Mason jars are taller than they are wide, so kombucha brewed in Mason jars may take longer than kombucha brewed in wider containers, and you may wind up with slightly higher levels of alcohol.

To simplify the kombucha-making process, you may want a jar or barrel with a spigot installed near the bottom. Wood spigots are sometimes available; otherwise, you might be happy with a plastic spigot. If you do use a plastic spigot, find one that is food safe and manufactured in a country with consumer protection and regulations (for example, the United States, not China). Plastic spigots are less problematic than plastic jugs because spigots have much less surface area. Nonetheless, purists may still balk at having acidic liquids in long-term contact with plastic of any sort. Siphon pumps and hoses are a possible alternative to spigots. And it's entirely possible to brew kombucha without spigots or pumps, albeit at some cost in convenience and fizz, by pouring rather than siphoning or spigotting. (See chapter 7 on page 98 for more on kombucha.)

SAFETY AND SANITATION

Beginning fermenters sometimes worry about food poisoning and microbiological safety.

The safety concerns fall into two general categories. First, many of us have heard stories about improperly canned foods leading to potentially fatal cases of botulism. The concern with canned foods is real, although the number of actual incidents is pretty low. Every year in the United States, between 100 and 200 cases of botulism are reported and confirmed, and more probably go unidentified or unreported. Canned foods, whether canned at home or in factories, must be produced deliberately and methodically. The good news is that very specific procedures have been documented describing how to produce canned foods safely; if these procedures are followed closely, major problems are very, very unlikely. The even better news is that fermenting resembles canning only superfi-

cially. Both are food preserving techniques and both often involve Mason jars, but that's where the similarities end. Canning involves destroying all the microbes, generally with heat, pressure, and chemicals, while fermenting involves supporting some microbes, discouraging others, and playing the first group against the second, by lowering the pH, controlling access to oxygen, and more subtly varying temperature. Canning is a massacre, while fermenting is a war of attrition and diplomacy. Fermenters' problems are quite different from canners'. Canning's greatest scourge, botulism, is not an issue for fermenters, in large part because of the lower pH involved in fermentation.

Second, fermenting goes against our refrigerator training. "Put it back in the refrigerator when you're done," our parents would repeat. We must untrain ourselves a bit if we wish to ferment. To everything there is a season, including refrigeration. It's important to understand that refrigeration slows down the fermentation processes that we're interested in. Sometimes, we do want to slow down these processes, but most of the time we don't. Temperature is something we can adjust strategically.

Sanitation is another place where canning and fermenting differ. Canning best practices dictate that we boil jars and lids before we use them and then boil everything for specific periods of time during the process, possibly under pressure to achieve an even higher temperature. Fermenting is more forgiving; it's important to maintain a clean workspace but it need not be spotless. Jars and bottles should be free of foreign objects, insects in particular. Glass may be sterilized with hot or boiling water if desired, but it's not necessary. Mason jars are designed to be immersed in boiling water, put in the dishwasher, or washed by hand; any of these is adequate. Boiling is often the best option for cleaning small-necked jugs, but again, it's not necessary.

In general, use mild, low-residue, unscented dish soap or dishwasher powder. Low-residue soap should be used on hands, too. Many green brands are good, although some of them are "green" in marketing only and contain harsh detergents or strong "natural" scents that take hours to dissipate!

Antibacterial soaps are particularly problematic. If they aren't rinsed off hands and equipment completely, they can lead to failed ferments. Worse yet, some antibacterial soaps contain dangerous toxic ingredients such as triclosan. Do you remember in chapter 1 when we mentioned that humans are giant bags of microbes? Our overall health is a function of the health, diversity, and balance of our collections of microbes. Unconsciously poisoning these microbes can lead to a myriad of mysterious maladies. Antibacterial soaps generally don't even do a good job at what they're trying to do—they just wipe out some subset of the microbes they come across. The best advice is to stay away from antibacterial soap completely, whether or not you're fermenting! In fact, triclosan, a common antibacterial ingredient, is now banned in soaps in parts of the United States and will hopefully continue to be banned more widely. Triclosan and antibacterial soaps were a victory of marketing over science and public health. They've been in consumer products for decades, and regulators are only now deciding that maybe they do more harm than good.

There are a few pieces of brewing equipment that are hard to clean and can't go in a dishwasher, such as siphon pumps and tubing. Homebrew stores sell chemical sanitizing liquids for cleaning these sorts of things. Commercial brewers may not have many other options. But for home purposes, running white vinegar through these and then flushing them well with water should suffice, with no risks to our health or to our ferments.

59

MISCELLANEOUS

YOU MAY NEED THE FOLLOWING:

- A large wooden spoon
- A ladle small enough to fit inside a wide mouth Mason jar
- Large mixing bowls (stainless steel is light, durable, easy to wash)
- Fruit fly traps
- Fly swatters
- Kitchen towels

As you become an experienced fermenter, you will discover other tools that can help you in various ways. Everyone has their favorites.

The fruit fly trap is a useful device. Fruit flies are attracted to various ferments, including anything involving fruit juice, kombucha, or vinegar. (See "The Drunken Monkey" on page 28.)

To make a fruit fly trap, fill a small (4-ounce [125 ml] or 8-ounce [250 ml]) Mason jar halfway with vinegar or kombucha and add one drop of dish soap; then, put a paper towel or coffee filter over the top, secure it with a canning lid ring, and punch several smallish holes in the paper top. When the flies become intrigued by the delicious smell in the jar, they'll go through the holes and dive into the liquid. Because the soap decreases the surface tension of the liquid and coats their wings, they perish. (The traps get gross. Make fresh ones as needed.)

Fly swatters can be useful too. Recently, electric fly swatters have become available. They look like a cross between a tennis racket and a bug zapper. They are effective, oddly satisfying to use, and also help build hand-eye coordination.

It is worth mentioning that you don't want to use toxic insecticide spray near your food. (Or anywhere, really.)

(A) *stainless steel bowls and a spatula,* (B) *du-rag,* (C) *candy thermometer and wide-mouth Mason jar,* (D) *pineapple spiralizer,* (E) *small mesh strainer,* (F) *ladle,* (G) *chef's knife,* (H) *lemon zester,* (I) *vegetable grater,* (J) *wooden spoon,* (K) *syphon with hose,* (L) *larger mesh strainer,* (M) *stainless steel funnels,* (N) *vegetable peeler*

WATER

Water is a key to human life. Much municipal tap water contains impurities, which vary from place to place and from time to time. They can be viewed as belonging to three categories: unintentional toxic impurities, intentional impurities, and (often beneficial) trace minerals.

Unintentional toxic impurities include heavy metals (lead, mercury, and cadmium), biological contaminants (spores and protozoa), and chemical residues from pesticides, herbicides, and prescription pharmaceuticals. We are all better off without these.

Intentional impurities are added to water during the purification process. Some of these impurities, generally chlorine and chlorine derivatives, are intended to inhibit the growth of microbes. For water in transit, this makes some sense. But once it reaches your house, it has served its purpose. Chlorine in various forms will inhibit the growth of the microbes in your ferments. It will also inhibit the growth of desirable microbes in your gut and on your body.

Trace minerals are left in the water during the purification process. Some trace minerals can be healthful, although we don't need to get them from drinking water—we can find them elsewhere.

Actively filtering your water is the best way to address both unintentional and intentional impurities. Water filters range from simple plastic pitchers to elaborate whole-house setups, with many options to choose from in between. The best strategy is to contact your local water authority and ask them what sorts of impurities your water might contain, and then gauge your filtering strategy accordingly. Reputable filter manufacturers will be able to tell you what their filters are good at and what they're not good at.

Having said all that, any filter is better than no filter. If a pitcher-type filter is what's manageable for you, then use one. They are quite effective for some kinds of water additives, although they are not effective for chloramine, a form of chlorine that more and more water authorities are starting to use, and they are also not helpful for removing fluoride, another contaminant often added to our water without our consent.

If it's completely impractical for you to filter your water, don't. But if your ferments fail to thrive, water problems may be one of the reasons. Boiling water and then cooling it can remove or neutralize some sorts of additives, although contrary to popular belief, it won't quickly remove all forms of chlorine.

SUGAR

YOU MAY USE THE FOLLOWING:

- White granulated cane sugar
- Brown sugar
- Raw sugar, Demerara sugar, Muscovado, Turbinado, or Sucanat
- Panela, piloncillo, or jaggery
- Molasses
- Coconut sugar
- Honey
- Maple syrup
- Aguamiel de maguey

Sugar, in one form or another, is an important ingredient in most fermented beverage recipes. That's because sugar is central to the chemical reactions involved in fermentation. Most of it gets transformed into something else during the fermentation, so don't be alarmed when the kombucha recipe calls for a full cup (200 g) of white sugar. The sugar is food for the microbes, not for you, and it will mostly be gone by the time you drink the kombucha. For more about the chemical reactions involved in fermentation, see chapter 3 on page 34.

Artificial sweeteners such as aspartame, saccharine, and sucralose cannot take the place of sugar in these recipes. Microbes can't digest these sweeteners. Neither can humans, generally; we would do well to take our cue from the microbes. Natural non-caloric sweeteners such as stevia also won't work. Microbes want actual sugar, period, although it doesn't have to be white sugar.

Powdered sugar is not a good choice because it generally contains cornstarch to keep it from clumping. You probably don't want cornstarch in your ferments, although it might not ruin things. And if you are trying to avoid GMO, then definitely avoid the cornstarch, since most corn is genetically modified; and opt for cane sugar over beet sugar, since most beet sugar comes from genetically modified beets.

As far as sugar and its relatives go, the lighter the color, the purer it is. Purity sounds like a good thing, but in this case, it isn't always. Much of the time, we're better off with darker, less refined sugar or darker liquid sweeteners such as maple syrup, molasses, and aguamiel de maguey. They are dark because they contain minerals, often in easily assimilated forms. They are all mostly sugar, so fermentation can happen just fine.

Making fermented drinks with unrefined sugars is one way to get more minerals in our diets. When the sugar is digested by the microbes, the minerals are left behind for us. In fact, fermentation is a way to get a good dose of minerals without all the sugar that they were originally paired with—a much higher ratio of minerals to sugar than they had in their original form. (And assuming our kidneys are working properly and we're drinking enough liquids, it's very unlikely that we'll overwhelm our bodies with minerals.)

(A) *panela (piloncillo),* (B) *maple syrup,* (C) *turbinado sugar,* (D) *aguamiel de maguey,* (E) *brown sugar,* (F) *raw honey,* (G) *white sugar*

These days, it's easy for us to fail to get the dietary minerals we need. There are a few factors that contribute to our mineral deficits. One is that modern soil fertilization techniques fail to replenish some of the trace minerals in the soil. Minerals are not metabolized or destroyed by our bodies; they pass through or are assimilated into tissues and bones. In the old days, manure and corpses from animals and even from humans all went back into the soil—things operated in a closed loop. In the time since industrialization and the advent of large-scale animal confinement, manure went from being an asset to being a water-polluting liability. Our new fossil fuel–based fertilizers don't have as high mineral content as the fertilizer that we used to get for free.

64

Another reason we may fail to get all our minerals has to do with modern grain preparation. Traditional preparation often involved long periods of soaking and fermenting, which neutralized mineral-blocking compounds in grains, such as phytic acid. Modern, "quick" grain preparation techniques do not counter these antinutritious compounds, so we are often less able to extract the minerals that we need from our foods.

A third reason for mineral shortfalls is the modern Standard American Diet—one of the United States' many successful cultural exports! A lot of us consume empty calories these days. Processed foods, sodas, and commercial baked goods seldom contain their share of interesting nutrients. They are made up of starches and/or refined sugars, refined salt, unhealthy fats of one sort or another (usually industrially produced vegetable oils, often toxically processed, with residues of solvents), and chemical flavorings and colorings and preservatives of various sorts. The more processed food we eat, the less room we have in our diets and in our stomachs for nutrient-dense foods.

Finally, we get depleted by the constant social and physical stresses of jobs and modern life, combined with the environmental stressors of pollution. And remember how piloting two-ton fortresses complicates our relationship with alcohol? Our bodies were not designed to be in the ongoing state of stress and heightened alert that are part and parcel of modern industrial life, including driving cars. It raises our cortisol levels and increases our nutritional require-ments. So just at the time in history when we could use more nutrition, we are getting less.

The upshot of all this is that we would all do well to gather our minerals while we may. A few of the recipes in this book require a specific sweetener for reasons of tradition or categorization (mead is not mead unless it's made with honey), but most of the recipes are not very picky. Fermenting provides us an opportunity to benefit from the minerals found in a variety of sugars and juices without having to consume a lot of sugar. And there are times we may want to use plain white sugar, and that's okay too.

Some of the sugar sources that can be used in these recipes include the ones listed here. Many of them are available in organic forms, which is generally preferable. Note that some forms of sugar are known by multiple names—food naming is not perfectly standardized, especially across different regions.

Most sweeteners are denser than white sugar, and most are less sweet. Thus, if you are measuring by volume, you could use a smaller measure of another sweetener than you might of sugar, but if you are measuring by weight, you could use more. The ratios are not hard and fast; analyze the nutrition labels on your sweeteners, if you like. A better plan, regardless of anything else, may be to use an amount of sweetener comparable to the amount of sugar called for in the recipe; take notes; see how your batch turns out; and then adjust as you see fit next time.

FIVE-MINUTE RECIPES

CHAPTER FIVE

You may think that you don't have time to make fermented beverages.

But you would be wrong!

SWEET LASSI   **69**

SALTY OR
SAVORY LASSI   **71**

DOOGH   **72**

SALTY FERMENTED
LEMONADE   **73**
OR LIMEADE

SWITCHEL   **74**

SEKANJABIN   **75**

To get you started in the world of fermented drinks, here are some simple recipes that you can put together quickly. Once you have all the ingredients, the recipes themselves are trivial. The fermented ingredients you'll be using include the following:

- Plain full-fat yogurt, store-bought or homemade (see page 86), or Milk Kefir (see page 88)

- Raw, unfiltered apple cider vinegar, store-bought or homemade (see page 95)

- Preserved lemons, store-bought or homemade (see recipe in *Real Food Fermentation*, or on the Internet)

HONEY IN THE RAW

Some of the recipes in this section call for raw honey. It's easiest to mix the honey into drinks if it's dissolved in a little warm water first. But be careful: If the water is too hot, the honey will no longer be raw, and cooked honey is less nutritious.

The temperature at which cooking starts is around 118°F (48°C)—this is where enzymes (which are proteins) start to change their shape, rendering them inactive, generally permanently. Not coincidentally, this is also the temperature at which your finger starts to hurt if you put it in hot water: It is to our advantage to know when we are getting cooked, and we have evolved to know when it's happening! So, if you're making drinks to be consumed immediately, you can use the finger test for temperature. Or if you're saving the drinks for later or sharing them with other people, you could grab a kitchen thermometer instead. (Some people might prefer not to have your fingers in their drinks!)

5-MINUTE FERMENTED VEGETABLE JUICES

You can make potent digestive tonics from fermented vegetables such as raw sauerkraut, kimchi, and pickles. Look for them at your grocery store or ferment them yourself using recipes from the Internet or books such as *Real Food Fermentation*. If you have a juicer, simply juice them! Or use a blender to blend them and then press the purée through a fine-mesh strainer with a mixing bowl underneath to collect the liquid. Serve this resulting liquid, mixed with sparkling water if you like. See page 116 for more details.

SWEET LASSI

Lassi is a yogurt drink popular on the Indian subcontinent. Served chilled, it's light, frothy, and immensely refreshing. Make it plain, sweeten it, or add savory flavors (see page 71). Once you've mastered the method, start adjusting the amount of various ingredients to suit yourself or your family and friends. If you hit on a particularly inspiring combination, don't forget to write it down!

Lassi is an easy path to drinkable yogurt. The only equipment you'll need for the most basic, fruit-free version is a Mason jar large enough to hold everything with at least an inch (2.5 cm) of room to spare at the top. Using Mason jars makes cleanup easy since they can go in the dishwasher. And if you have a blender, fruit lassis are easy too. (In fact, the threads on some blender jars match the threads on standard mouth Mason jars. If you have one of these blenders, you can explore blending directly in your Mason jar.)

YIELD: ABOUT 2 SERVINGS (8 OUNCES, OR 250 ML, EACH)

1 cup (225 g) plain full-fat yogurt, store-bought or homemade

1 cup (250 ml) water and/or high-quality, full-fat milk

A few ice cubes

If not using fruit, up to 2 teaspoons (10 g) granulated sugar, (15 g) raw honey, maple syrup, or aguamiel de maguey

WITHOUT FRUIT

Place the yogurt, water, ice, sugar, salt, and cardamom (if using) in a Mason jar. Close the lid tightly. Shake vigorously until frothy. The ice helps with the frothing; to make it frothier and lighter, add at least ¼ cup (60 ml) more water and shake more vigorously.

Remove the lid and serve. If you don't serve it all at once, shake again immediately before serving the rest.

(continued next page)

69

Pinch of sea salt

¹⁄₈ teaspoon ground cardamom (optional)

Pulp of 1 mango (about 1 cup [175 g]) or 1 cup (175 g) chopped fresh pineapple (optional)

WITH FRUIT

Blend the yogurt, water, ice, salt, cardamom (if using) and mango or pineapple in a blender on high speed for about 30 seconds or until nice and frothy. If not completely blended, repeat until smooth. Serve with more ice if desired.

SALTY OR SAVORY LASSI

These lassis are great with meals. Adjust the spices based on where you live, what's available, and what you like. Try the curry powder if you like. Ginger is refreshing, turmeric will give your drink a wonderful orange color, and cumin adds intense flavor. Mint and cucumber are a great summer combination; try five-spice powder or cinnamon in the winter. All the individual spices have specific health benefits, and yogurt and spices can help your digestion!

**YIELD: ABOUT 2 SERVINGS
(8 OUNCES, OR 250 ML, EACH)**

1 cup (225 g) plain full-fat yogurt, store-bought or homemade

1 cup (250 ml) water mixed with about $\frac{1}{4}$ cup (60 g) crushed ice

Pinch of sea salt

SEASONING OF YOUR CHOICE
(CHOOSE FROM THE FOLLOWING):

1 teaspoon curry powder, or to taste

1 teaspoon five-spice powder, or to taste

$\frac{1}{4}$ teaspoon ground cumin, or to taste

$\frac{1}{4}$ teaspoon ground fennel seed, or to taste

1 teaspoon powdered turmeric or fresh turmeric grated extra-fine with a microplane or zester, or to taste

Place the yogurt, water, salt, and seasoning in a Mason jar. Close the lid tightly. Shake vigorously until frothy. The ice helps with the frothing; to make it frothier and lighter, add at least $\frac{1}{4}$ cup (60 ml) water and shake more vigorously.

Remove the lid and serve. If you don't serve it all at once, shake again immediately before serving the rest.

71

DOOGH

Doogh is similar to lassi in that it's a savory yogurt-based drink. The biggest difference between doogh, which has its roots in ancient Persia, and lassi is that doogh should be fizzy—this is why we make it with sparkling water. It's a refreshing, easy way to introduce probiotic drinks into your diet.

This recipe is a shortcut version. If you're feeling bold, we encourage you to try the traditional Iranian recipe: Make homemade yogurt and then let it sit for several weeks at room temperature in a jar or bottle with an airtight lid. When it starts getting bubbly, it's ready. You can find a homemade yogurt recipe on page 94.

**YIELD: 2 SERVINGS
(8 OUNCES, OR 250 ML, EACH)**

1 cup (225 g) plain full-fat yogurt
or Milk Kefir (see page 88)

½ teaspoon dried mint

Pinch of sea salt

Pinch of ground black pepper

1 cup (250 ml) sparkling
or mineral water

1 cup (250 g) ice cubes or crushed ice

Fresh mint leaves (optional)

Stir the yogurt, mint, salt, and pepper in a quart (1 L) Mason jar until the mint, salt, and pepper are distributed evenly throughout the yogurt. Add the sparkling water and stir just enough to blend well. (The more you stir, the more bubbles you'll lose.) It will look like smooth, bubbly liquid yogurt.

Divide the ice between two glasses. Pour the doogh over the ice. Garnish with fresh mint leaves (if using) and serve.

SALTY FERMENTED LEMONADE OR LIMEADE

Salty lemonade is nature's sports drink. It contains the electrolytes and trace minerals that we need when sweating, along with a bit of sugar that can be helpful for keeping our energy up. And if it's made with preserved lemons (or limes), it provides the health and digestive benefits of fermented foods too.

Many cultures enjoy lemonade or limeade. This recipe is closest to the Vietnamese version, Soda Chanh, which is salty and sparkly and features mint leaves. As you make it again and again, try dialing back the amount of sweetener. Learn to enjoy the balance between sweet and sour rather than just the sugar rush!

YIELD: 1 SERVING (8 OUNCES, OR 250 ML)

1/8 of a salty preserved lemon in brine or 1/4 or a salty preserved lime in brine (find a recipe in *Real Food Fermentation* or on the Internet)

Sweetener of your choice, to taste (start with 1 teaspoon natural sugar or raw honey)

A few mint leaves (optional)

Crushed ice

1 cup (250 ml) sparkling or still water

Aggressively muddle the preserved lemon (or lime), sweetener, mint leaves (if using), and ice with a drink muddler, mortar and pestle, blender, or whatever means convenient. It does not have to be completely uniform. Add the water and stir. Serve in a tall glass with a straw.

SWITCHEL

Switchel belongs to the family of vinegar- or wine-based drinks that has been around since Classical Greek times or before. (See chapter 2 on page 26.) A popular colonial-era drink in the United States, it is experiencing something of a comeback in the twenty-first century. It traditionally features apple cider vinegar and maple syrup, but the only truly required ingredients are vinegar and water, so let's try some interesting (and delicious!) variations. This version adds ginger and a bit of sweetener. For a tropical twist, use pineapple tepache vinegar and aguamiel de maguey.

For the greatest health benefits, make sure to use raw, unfiltered vinegar. Switchel made with pasteurized vinegar is not a fermented drink, and it will be missing microbes, enzymes, and vitamins. Molasses works well in this recipe, and it has a great mineral profile.

**YIELD: ABOUT 4 SERVINGS
(8 OUNCES, OR 250 ML, EACH)**

3 tablespoons (60 g) maple syrup, aguamiel de maguey, molasses, or raw honey

3 tablespoons (45 ml) raw, unfiltered apple cider or pineapple tepache vinegar, store-bought or homemade (see page 178)

1 teaspoon grated fresh ginger

Juice of ½ of a lime (optional)

1 quart (1 L) filtered water

Place all the ingredients in a half gallon (2 L) Mason jar. Close the lid tightly and shake well. Refrigerate overnight and/or serve over ice.

VARIATION: Mix all the ingredients except for the water. This can be done ahead of time, and the resulting syrup can be stored in the refrigerator for a week or more. When ready to serve, pour 1 ounce (30 ml) of syrup into a glass over a few ice cubes and add 7 ounces (200 ml) of sparkling water. The result is a nice probiotic soda alternative.

SEKANJABIN

Sekanjabin is a popular drink in Iran, where it is served over ice during the summer. It's a flawless combination of sweet and sour, and it's immensely refreshing—ideal for anyone who wants to add microbes to his or her diet. Once you've made the sekanjabin syrup, it only takes a few minutes to prepare the drink, and the syrup itself lasts for months.

YIELD: ABOUT
1½ GALLONS (6 L)

4 cups (800 g) organic granulated sugar

2½ cups (625 ml) filtered water

½ cup (50 g) fresh mint leaves or ¼ cup (30 g) grated fresh ginger, depending on desired flavor

1 cup (250 ml) raw, unfiltered red or white wine vinegar

Dissolve the sugar in the water in a medium-size pot over medium heat, stirring occasionally. Once simmering, add the mint leaves. Simmer, uncovered, until the syrup thickens, about 10 to 15 minutes. Remove from the heat and let cool to room temperature. Strain out the solids with a strainer. Add the vinegar. Store at room temperature in a well-sealed container such as a Mason jar.

To prepare the drink, stir 2 tablespoons (30 ml) of syrup into 1 cup (250 ml) of cold water.

STARTERS, MASTER RECIPES, AND GENERAL PRINCIPLES

Humans have been fermenting, thinking about fermentation, and attempting to troubleshoot ferments throughout recorded history. Our understanding of the process reflects the natural science of our time and our culture. Today, we explain it using microbes and chemical reactions. Traditional explanations of fermentation may have included ideas about plant spirits or about forces attached to specific vessels in which things ferment, and ways that these forces can travel from one vessel to another.

MASTER RECIPE: **83**
GINGER BUG

MASTER RECIPE: **86**
YOGURT

MASTER RECIPE: **88**
MILK KEFIR

MASTER RECIPE: **91**
WHEY

MASTER RECIPE: **95**
VINEGAR

MASTER RECIPE: **96**
WATER KEFIR

These ideas might sound like superstition to our modern ears, but they have been just as useful to their proponents as our explanations are to us. And we can't know how our current explanations will sound to humans a thousand years from now!

THE BEST MICROBES FOR THE JOB: BACTERIA VS. YEAST VS. MOLD

One of the first things to determine about any fermentation project is what sorts of microbes are involved: bacteria, yeast, or mold.

Bacteria are microscopic, single-celled organisms. (And lest you think that saying both "microscopic" and "single-celled" is redundant, consider that a chicken egg is a single cell!) Bacteria are neither plants nor animals, and they were among the first forms of life. A typical human body is host to hundreds of trillions of bacterial cells, most of which reside in the gut.

Many bacteria produce lactic acid as part of their metabolism. Lactic acid–producing bacteria, or *lactic acid bacteria* (LABs) for short, can be found in plants and milk products, in the air, in our bodies, and in other places. LABs are notable for their ability to tolerate acidic conditions. Many other sorts of bacteria do not tolerate acidic conditions—including many of the bacteria that are potentially harmful to us

humans. LABs produce acid that inhibits the growth of these harmful bacteria, thus contributing to the long-term safety of fermented foods. That's why LABs are known as friendly bacteria. Especially in colder climates, where fresh food is less available year-round, LABs and lactic acid fermentation (lactofermentation) have been important to human foodways because of the roles they can play in preserving food. Lactic acid ferments include all but a few cheeses, all sour dairy products, and most traditional sour preparations, including sour vegetables. Vinegars involve primarily acetic acid bacteria; their story is similar to the story of LABs.

Yeasts are also single-celled organisms, more complicated and physically larger than bacteria. Members of the fungi kingdom, their special talent is producing alcohol; most alcoholic drinks involve yeast in some way. They also produce carbon dioxide, which is why they make drinks bubble and bread rise. Yeasts have been key to the human relationship with wheat especially, but also with honey, grapes, apples, and other fruits. Thanks to yeasts, bread and beer are two of the most important forms of preserved wheat. Mead, wine, cider, and other fruit wines also involve yeast. Stronger alcoholic drinks have yeast-fermented drinks as starting points; these are concentrated via distillation.

Molds are also fungi. They're biologically similar to yeasts in some ways, but they grow in multicellular clumps. Molds play roles in the creation some kinds of cheeses: in the bodies of blue cheeses and a few others and in the rinds of most soft cheeses. Molds also play roles in dry-cured meats and in some grain and legume preserves such as miso, sake, and soy sauce.

Some ferments rely on a combination of bacteria and yeast, often referred to as a SCOBY, which is an acronym for Symbiotic Community (or Culture) of Bacteria and Yeast. (Sometimes the term *colony* is used rather than *community*; *colony* isn't quite accurate in this context because it generally implies a homogeneous collection, and a SCOBY by definition contains variety.)

SCOBY is also often used to refer to a visible manifestation of the microbes—in the case of kombucha, a cellulosic mat that floats on top of the brew. (Vinegar has a similar SCOBY that's generally called mother of vinegar. It may or may not float on top.) *SCOBY* as the visible part of the ferment is common usage, but it can mislead newcomers into thinking that all the microbes live in the mat, which isn't the case. Some SCOBY ferments, such as kefir, don't have a mat at all, but have small globules instead.

STARTERS AND HOW TO GET THEM

A starter is something that you add to a fermentable substrate to encourage it to ferment in a particular way. Some fermentation projects don't require starters at all, consistently fermenting the way you want them to if the temperature, surface area, salt, availability of oxygen, and so on are approximately right. Other ferments require a starter. And yet others can be done with or without a starter.

Given a choice, it is more exciting to ferment without a starter, or with a homemade starter, because the results can be pleasantly surprising. But they can also be unpleasantly surprising, so if you are depending on your ferment, needing to meet a deadline or using it for economic gain, for instance, you may want to take the route of less uncertainty by using a starter.

SCOBY STARTERS

The most common SCOBY ferments are kombucha (and its cousin jun), vinegar, milk kefir (*búlgaros*), and water kefir (*tíbicos*).

In order to make a SCOBY ferment, in most cases, you need a starter, which usually consists of the physical manifestation of the SCOBY plus some of the fermented liquid.

These days, it's easy to buy any of these starters on the Internet. The best place to find them may change from time to time; check the "Resources" section of our website www.KombuchaKefirandBeyond.com for up-to-date recommendations.

If you'd like to get one for free, ask your friends! Or look at the various culture sharing sites and groups on the Internet that can help you find donors. Again, check the "Resources" section of our website for good recommendations.

Vinegar is one SCOBY ferment for which you don't need a starter. *Acetobacter*, the bacteria that are key to making vinegar, are widespread, and they are good at finding open vessels of wine, cider, tepache, and other alcohol ferments and turning them into vinegar. So, you can make vinegar without getting a starter; it will do fine without one. You may even find yourself having made vinegar by accident! Generally, all you need to do is leave an alcohol ferment exposed to the air—ideally covered with a cloth to keep bugs out. (Some vinegar recipes recommend courting flies to capture the *Acetobacter* that they carry and then straining out the dead flies later, but this is quite unnecessary!)

BACTERIAL STARTERS

In most cases in this book, we make our own bacterial starters (e.g., Ginger Bug on page 83) or else we do not use starters at all (e.g., Beet Kvass on page 118).

One case in which a starter is necessary is yogurt. Fortunately, you can start yogurt with a small portion of active culture, high-quality plain yogurt! That means that a yogurt starter is available in most grocery stores and even some convenience stores.

Vegetable fermentation starters are not generally necessary for ferments such as Beet Kvass (see page 118) and sauerkraut. But if we are attempting to ferment vegetables under less than ideal conditions, such as at a temperature above 85°F (30°C) or with less than the ideal amount of salt, we may choose to use a bacterial starter. For sources of vegetable fermentation starters, again, check the "Resources" section of our website, or simply search online for "vegetable starter culture."

YEAST STARTERS

Some yeast projects, such as tepache, do not require yeast starters. Others, including wine and cider, will turn out more consistently when yeast starters are used. The result with a starter can be more predictable, although while avoiding the failures, you may miss out on the occasional fantastic surprise.

Yeast starters can be bought at homebrew stores or on the Internet. They can also be captured by exposing sweet liquids to air and stirring them a lot, and from the surface of fresh, unsprayed fruit such as apples, grapes, and berries. Once you have created a bubbly starter this way, you can add it to your bigger batch of fermentable liquid. This is an in-between strategy, not as predictable as using yeast from an envelope, but less uncertain than starting a big batch without a starter at all.

FERMENTATION, AIR, AND BUBBLES

Fermentations can either be performed with access to ambient air (ideally covered with a cloth or a coffee filter to keep insects out!) or with no access to ambient air (either completely sealed or with an airlock or one-way valve of some sort allowing an outflow of gas but no backflow).

If you want *Acetobacter* to find your drink, your drink will need to be open to the air. If you are counting on having wild yeast find your drink, it's the same story. (In these cases, you

will need a fine cloth, coffee filter, or paper towel to keep any bugs out.) Conversely, when you don't want your drink to become more sour, you will want to cut off access to air to keep *Aceto-bacter* under control. Some projects go through phases in which you will do each of these things in turn. And in fact, kombucha seems to do both on its own; at some point during the process, the kombucha SCOBY settles at the top of the drink and forms a pretty good seal.

The other side of the air issue is the question of carbonation. While things are fermenting, they generate some amount of carbon dioxide gas. This gas can be harnessed to make your beverage bubbly. To capture bubbles, seal a container tightly while fermentation is actively happening. You can accomplish this by sealing its original fermenting vessel or by moving the drink to new vessels, perhaps smaller, that can be easily sealed.

Carbonation escapes once a bottle is open, so if you are aiming for carbonation, you may want to bottle directly into serving-size containers (bottles or jars). And once your drink has achieved the desired level of carbonation, you may want to put it in the refrigerator. This does two things. First, it greatly slows (but does not stop) the ongoing fermentation, rendering your drink more stable. Second, it allows more of the gas to dissolve in the liquid because carbon dioxide, like most gasses, dissolves better in liquids at lower temperatures—this makes your drink more bubbly and also makes it even more stable.

When bottling, you have the option to add some more sugar, either in the form of actual sugar or in the form of fruit or dried fruit. When you seal the bottle, the sugar continues to ferment. This in-bottle fermentation is called secondary fermentation, or 2f for short.

Some care must be taken when fermenting things in sealed containers. It's important to use only bottles that have been designed with carbonation and pressure in mind. This means that beer bottles, kombucha bottles, champagne bottles, and even plastic soda bottles are fine, but wine bottles may not be.

Even when taking these precautions, bottles can occasionally explode. You don't want glass bottles exploding; it's messy and potentially dangerous. There are a couple of things that you can do to avoid explosions:

- Be conservative and make changes gradually. It's hard to make sweeping statements about how much sugar to add during 2f of kombucha. But you may want to start with 4 raisins or frozen blueberries per bottle and see how that goes. If that's not enough, try 6. Again, it's hard to give hard-and-strict formulas with so many variables—variables such as ambient temperature, residual sugar in your kombucha, and the strength of your kombucha culture.

- Use one plastic bottle along with any glass bottles you are using. Choose a plastic bottle that is a similar size to the glass bottles and fill it similarly full. As pressure builds up, you can test the plastic bottle by squeezing it. When it becomes hard like a soda bottle, you probably have a good amount of carbonation, and it may be time to put all your bottles in the refrigerator (or drink them!).

GINGER BUG

A ginger bug is a great, easy-to-make starter for a bacterial/sour ferment of almost anything containing sugar. Sugary liquids left to their own devices often go in a yeast/alcohol direction, but the bug can help steer them away from this. It works particularly well in coconut water.

So why a *ginger* bug? Why not a celery bug or potato bug? To find out, Raquel asked her friend Ernesto Fato, a chemical engineer from the beautiful state of Oaxaca, Mexico, who lives and works in Monterrey in the food and beverage industry. He is Raquel's helping hand and brains, especially when something doesn't quite turn out the way she expects in her kitchen lab. Ernesto's conclusion was that good quality raw ginger provides an excellent substrate for the growth of lactic acid bacteria, while at the same time inhibiting the growth of other bacteria. *Gracias Ernesto!*

**YIELD: I PINT (500 ML)
ACTIVE GINGER BUG**

STARTER INGREDIENTS

2 cups (500 ml) filtered water

2 tablespoons (20 g)
grated raw organic ginger

2 tablespoons (30 g)
organic granulated sugar

Stir the starter ingredients in a Mason jar until the sugar is dissolved. Cover the jar with a clean cloth, kitchen towel, paper towel, or coffee filter and secure it with a rubber band or Mason jar ring. Write the date on a piece of masking tape and stick it to the outside of the jar.

To feed the bug: Each subsequent day, grate 1 tablespoon (10 g) of ginger, uncover the jar, add 1 tablespoon (15 g) of sugar and the freshly grated ginger, stir vigorously, and cover the jar as before. After about a week, give or take

(continued next page)

At least 4 tablespoons (30 g)
raw organic ginger

A least 4 tablespoons (50 g)
sugar, plus more to maintain

depending on temperature, the liquid will be bubbly. At this point, your ginger bug is alive and ready for action.

Once the bug is well established, it's no longer necessary to add more ginger. Continue feeding it a tablespoon (15 g) of sugar and stirring every day or two. It should remain fizzy. After a while, you will develop a feeling for how your feeding affects how bubbly it is. Before using it in a recipe, feed it more than usual to get it as bubbly as possible. If at some point it is no longer fizzy, this means that it is dead and will no longer work as a starter. In this case, make a new batch.

If you won't be able to feed it for a few days or longer, store it in the refrigerator, still covered with cloth or paper. When you are ready to revive it, leave it out at room temperature and resume feeding it daily. It may take a few days before it recovers fully. If it doesn't, start a new batch.

GINGER BUG TIPS & TRICKS

If a recipe calls for ginger bug to be used as a starter, only the liquid is necessary. Place a piece of tape on the outside of the jar to mark the level of liquid. Pour out however much you need, using a strainer if necessary. Refill the jar to the tape line with filtered water.

Avoid storing your ginger bug near other open container cultures such as kombucha—they can cross-contaminate, which leads to problems.

For a different flavor—and probably some different microbes—turmeric and galangal can be used in place of some or all the ginger.

YOGURT

In many places, it's possible to buy unsweetened, full-fat yogurt made from high-quality milk. But this hasn't always been the case, and it's still not everywhere. If you can get good milk but can't get good yogurt, you can make the yogurt yourself.

YIELD: 4 SERVINGS (8 OUNCES, OR 225 G, EACH)

1 tablespoon (15 ml) starter

1 quart (1 L) milk

One of the advantages of making it yourself is that you get to decide what goes in it. Many yogurts, even from "natural" brands, contain things other than milk and cultures. Another advantage is cost savings. It's hard to generalize about this, but it should almost always be cheaper to buy a gallon (4 L) of milk than four

OTHER EQUIPMENT OPTIONS

There are many other ways to keep yogurt at the right temperature while it ferments. One particularly convenient option is to place it in an oven with the oven light on. In many ovens, this will hold it at the right temperature. If you have an oven thermometer, you can test your oven:

Leave the light on for a while and then check the temperature—if it's between 95° F (35°C) and 110° F (43°C), you are all set. Follow the directions above, but use a 1 quart (1 L) Mason jar instead of a thermos and after closing the lid and shaking, put it in the oven with the oven light on.

You can also use a cooler. Add enough 110°F (43°C) water to the cooler to partially submerge the jar. Add the Mason jar holding the yogurt. Close the cooler and open it 12 to 24 hours later. The yogurt should be set.

quarts (4 kg) of yogurt. Yet another advantage is that homemade yogurt can be made to contain very little lactose, by fermenting it for longer than usual. (In theory, store-bought yogurt could be fermented more after purchase, too.)

Unhomogenized milk is best for making yogurt, if you can find it. Some brands of yogurt today are unhomogenized, and you can find unhomogenized milk at specialty stores. But if you can't manage unhomogenized, it's okay. You can easily make your own yogurt at home. You don't even need a fancy yogurt maker—you'll be good to go if you have a regular 1-quart (1 L) thermos and a candy thermometer or even just an oven with a lightbulb and some Mason jars. You will, however, need a culture starter, which can be any of the following:

- Whey from yogurt
- A previous batch of your own yogurt
- High-quality, plain store-bought yogurt, or yogurt starter (see "Resources" on page 200)
- Crème fraîche

Place the starter in a 1-quart (1 L) thermos.

Heat the milk in a large stainless steel pot fitted with a candy thermometer over medium heat until it reaches 180°F (82°C), but not too much hotter. Stir constantly with a wooden spoon to prevent boiling hot spots and scorching at the bottom of the pan. Once it reaches 180°F (82°C), you can turn the heat off and wait for it to cool. But if you hold it at 180°F (82°C) for a while, it will be thicker and creamier. If you are game, you can hold the resulting yogurt here for up to 20 or 30 minutes, stirring constantly.

Remove the pot from the heat and let the yogurt cool to about 110°F (43°C). If you're impatient, rest the pot in an ice bath. Stirring will also help it cool, as will moving it into a cold glass or ceramic container.

Once the yogurt reaches 110°F (43°C) or below, pour it into the thermos with the starter, close the lid, and shake. Do not let it get too far below 110°F (43°C) because that is the temperature at which these cultures thrive.

Write the date and time of preparation on the outside of the thermos. The longer the yogurt ferments, the sourer it will be and the less lactose it will contain. If you want your yogurt to be practically lactose-free, let it ferment for 24 hours. A more typical length of time is 8 to 12 hours.

Transfer the yogurt from the thermos to a heat-conductive container and refrigerate it.

MILK KEFIR

Likely originating in the Caucasus Mountains, milk kefir grains (*búlgaros de leche* in Spanish) are a SCOBY culture that ferments milk.

To make milk kefir, you must acquire a tablespoon (15 g) or so of these milk kefir grains, which look like cottage cheese or small cauliflower florets. (See "Resources" on page 200 for how to get a starter.) If you buy dehydrated grains, follow the instructions on the package to rehydrate them. Either way, you'll need a large glass or ceramic jar—Mason jars are ideal. Be aware that you will need an inch or two (2.5 to 5 cm) of headroom in the jar above the fermenting milk because kefir needs air while it's fermenting. If there's any question about what size jar to use, go larger rather than smaller.

**YIELD: 2 SERVINGS
(8 OUNCES, OR 250 ML, EACH)**

1 tablespoon (15 g)
dairy kefir grains

2 cups (500 ml) whole dairy
milk, raw or pasteurized

The milk kefir culture, like the yogurt culture, feeds on lactose, so it won't work with lactose-free milk. Fresh raw milk is the best because it contains lots of beneficial bacteria and enzymes of its own and will make a more biologically-diverse kefir. Make sure that it's no more than a day old; otherwise, the enzymes and microbes that naturally occur and multiply in raw milk can start to dominate the kefir microbes and send things in an unexpected direction, resulting in funky-tasting kefir and possibly a biological drift in the kefir grains, making them less effective in the future. Regular pasteurized milk works fine, too, or high-pressure processed milk if that's available where you are, but the same rule applies: the fresher the milk, the better.

Kefir ferments best at room temperature or warm room temperature. This makes it particularly convenient for people who live in rooms! In fact, it's even easier and more convenient to make than yogurt because it doesn't require elevated temperature, nor does it require the milk to be heated ahead of time.

Also, because kefir cultures tend to be "wilder" than yogurt cultures, in the sense that they contain more unknown strains of microbes, it's harder to generalize about things such as starter ratios, ideal temperatures, and times. For this reason, if you want to get consistent results, you may need to keep track of these parameters for yourself in a notebook or at least settle into a consistent routine and be conscious about varying it. For instance, you can put a piece of tape on the side of your kefir fermenting jar and always fill it with milk to the top of the tape.

If kefir is left to ferment for long enough, it will separate. You will see curds and whey. This kefir will be very sour, and may be past its prime for drinking, but it's still fine for smoothies, salad dressings, and so on.

Kefir probably contains a greater variety of microbes than yogurt. This means that it may be "more probiotic" than yogurt, although as with many matters of fermentation, it's hard to generalize with any certainty.

Place the kefir grains in a quart (1 L) Mason jar and pour the milk over them. Use a jar large enough to leave at least an inch (2.5 cm) of space at the top; if you're scaling up the recipe, then scale up the jar. Stir vigorously with a wooden or plastic spoon if necessary to get things mixed well. Seal with an airtight lid, or if you don't have any other SCOBY brews in the room, cover the top with a clean cloth, kitchen towel, paper towel, or coffee filter and secure with a rubber band or Mason jar ring. Agitate the milk mixture. Write the brewing date and time on a piece of masking tape and stick it to the outside of the jar.

FLAVOR YOUR MILK KEFIR

If you'd like some variety, add flavors such as vanilla or cinnamon to your kefir, to taste, right when you are drinking it, as you would when flavoring your coffee.

You can also add fruit for a secondary fermentation at room temperature with a sealed lid. For every cup (250 ml) of kefir, try ½ cup (100 g) fruit. Add the fruit to the kefir and then let it sit for up to a day at room temperature. Once it's ready, strain, if you like, and then refrigerate.

Let the kefir sit at room temperature for 12 to 24 hours. The first few times you make it, you may want to taste it to decide when it's done. It should be thick, sour, somewhat yeasty, and a bit wild, possibly with some barnyard funkiness!

Pour the kefir through a plastic or nylon strainer into a bowl or jar. Straining milk kefir can be confusing and stressful at first because the acidity of the kefir can cause the milk to curdle and/or proteins to coagulate more and more as it ferments. If you're having trouble distinguishing kefir grains from coagulated milk, don't hesitate to use your (clean!) fingers to pick through the globs, shake the strainer, or stir the grains in the strainer gently with a wooden or plastic spoon. Kefir grains will be firm to the touch, while the other things will not resist at all when you squeeze them. If necessary, you can pick out the kefir grains with your fingers and/or push the curdled milk globs through the strainer. Metal strainers and spoons are not recommended in any of this because they can cut the grains, making it harder to distinguish the grains from the kefir itself.

Your kefir is ready! Serve it now, or if you prefer it cold or want to save it for later, cover it and refrigerate it.

Transfer the kefir grains from the strainer to another glass or ceramic jar and start a new batch with them immediately, if possible. If you're not going to use your grains right away, store them in fresh milk in the refrigerator, covered, where they will be okay for weeks.

COCONUT WATER, COCONUT MILK, FRUIT JUICE, AND NUT MILK FERMENTS

Milk kefir grains can be used to culture coconut water or coconut milk, fruit juices, and nut milks. If you want to do this, we recommend that you alternate batches with milk because dairy kefir grains need lactose on a regular basis to remain healthy, and lactose is found only in dairy milk. We would even suggest two or three batches of dairy milk per batch of other liquids.

Fresh is better than canned or boxed. Juices are easy to make when you can get seasonal fruits from your local farmer's market.

Just substitute 2 cups (500 ml) coconut water, coconut milk, fruit juice, or nut milk for the dairy milk in this recipe and rinse the dairy kefir grains well with filtered water before beginning. Then proceed as you would with dairy milk.

WHEY

Little Miss Muffet • Sat on a tuffet • Eating her curds and whey

So goes the old English nursery rhyme. But have you ever wondered about curds and whey? What are they? These days, many of us have no direct experience with them. Under certain circumstances, liquid dairy products will separate into a more solid part, the curds, and a more liquid part, the whey. Conditions leading to this separation include an increase in acidity, the addition of enzymes, and sometimes other factors, such as being strained through cheesecloth.

**YIELD: VARIABLE;
1 QUART (1 L) OF YOGURT
MAY YIELD 1 PINT (500 ML)
OF WHEY AND 1 PINT (500 G)
OF STRAINED YOGURT**

Any amount plain,
full-fat, unsweetened yogurt
with live cultures

The whey portion contains a good amount of water and some whey protein; and if it comes from raw or fermented dairy, it also contains lactic acid–producing microbes. These microbes can be used for starting new ferments. Hence our interest in whey!

Note that for whey to be "alive," it must be made from raw or fermented dairy. Cheese-making also generates whey as a by-product, but most cheesemaking involves heating milk beyond 117°F (47°C), at which temperature the microbes start dying off; this "cooked" whey cannot reliably be used as a fermentation starter.

Whey can be used as a starter for ferment-ing vegetables, making drinks, or making other fermented dairy products. In some cases, such as when fermenting vegetables, adding whey is

91

optional—some people do it and others don't. In some other cases, such as when making yogurt, you need a starter, and whey from yogurt is a good one.

There are lots of ways to obtain whey. Two of the easiest are (1) leaving raw milk out at room temperature for between a day and a week, at which point it will sour and separate on its own, and (2) letting your milk kefir ferment until it separates on its own, which may take only a day or so.

Many of us don't have easy, immediate access to raw milk or to milk kefir. In this case, the easiest way to get whey is by straining dairy yogurt. To do so, you'll need something to strain it with—a clean nut milk bag, a kerchief, or a large fine-mesh cloth—and something to strain it into, such as a large mixing bowl or pitcher. David Asher suggests the kerchief in his book, *The Art of Natural Cheesemaking*.

Nourishing Traditions author Sally Fallon says that whey can keep for up to 6 months in the refrigerator. You'll know if it goes bad because things will start growing on the surface of it!

Place the yogurt in a nut milk bag or a fine-mesh cloth in such a way that you can tie it at the top.

Hang the yogurt-filled fabric over a large container to catch the drips: Tie it to a wooden spoon laid across the top of the container, a cabinet handle, or a fixture of some sort. You can even place the cloth on top of a strainer. Do this in a place where the yogurt won't be disturbed for a while. Do not squeeze it!

The watery liquid that drips into the container is whey. The yogurt that remains in the cloth is strained yogurt, Greek yogurt, yogurt cheese, or yogurt cream cheese, depending on what you want to call it and how long you strain it for. The longer it strains, the firmer it gets.

Pour the whey into a Mason jar. Write the date on a piece of masking tape and stick it to the outside of the jar. Cover tightly and refrigerate.

VINEGAR

Wines and other alcohol-fermented beverages turn into vinegar over time when exposed to oxygen. This means that vinegar is easy to make. Sometimes we make it without even meaning to! Bottle your finished vinegar in recycled wine or vinegar bottles or in Mason jars—vinegars are not fizzy, so there is no explosion risk. And making your second batch of vinegar can go quicker if you use some of your first batch as a starter; or you can use a store-bought raw vinegar instead as a starter if you like.

YIELD: VARIABLE

Wine or other alcohol-containing fermented beverage

¼ cup (60 ml) of existing raw vinegar per quart (liter) of wine (optional)

Pour the wine into a large open glass or ceramic vessel. To speed up the process, add ¼ cup (60 ml) raw vinegar (if using). Cover the vessel with a clean cloth, kitchen towel, paper towel, or coffee filter and secure it with a rubber band.

Let it sit at room temperature for a couple of weeks to a couple of months. After several weeks, you may see a mat forming on top. That is the vinegar mother.

Taste the vinegar from time to time. If it still tastes like wine (or whatever it started as), let it sit a few more weeks. If you like the taste, strain and bottle it. Cap and store at room temperature.

NOTE: Homemade vinegar made with this recipe is great for most culinary purposes. But if you need your vinegar for canning or for any other application where there is chemistry involved, then it is safer to use a store-bought vinegar, since these are standardized to particular levels of acidity.

WATER KEFIR
(TÍBICOS)

Water kefir is a quick ferment, only a day or two, involving both bacteria and yeast. It is dairy free, caffeine free, and a great alternative to sodas. It's fizzier than kombucha, easier and quicker to make, and less challenging flavor-wise. For these reasons, it can be a great first fermented drink, even for skeptics.

**YIELD: 4 SERVINGS
(8 OUNCES, OR 250 ML, EACH)**

¼ cup (50 g) sugar, such as piloncillo, cane sugar, or turbinado

1 quart (1 L) filtered water

2 tablespoons (30 g) hydrated water kefir grains

Rinsed and boiled shell of 1 egg, or 4 raisins, or 1 tablespoon (15 g) aguamiel de maguey for its excellent mineral content (optional)

¼ cup (50 g) chopped fruit or frozen berries for second fermentation (optional)

Water kefir grains are a SCOBY that digests sugar and creates acids. They do not require tea as do kombucha and Jun, only sugar. But to keep your kefir grains happy and growing, it is best to use darker sugar rather than plain white sugar. Piloncillo (also known as panela or rapadura) is a great option because it has a higher mineral content, which helps the grains reproduce. Some other good options include raw sugar, brown sugar, molasses, and aguamiel de maguey. Another way to get the necessary minerals is to include some raisins or other dried fruit. Yet another way is to include some boiled, crushed egg shells.

Water kefir grains can be bought or given to you for free. Buying them online is the most straightforward. There are also online communities and pages where you can trade cultures with other aficionados. (See "Resources" on page 200.) The grains risk starvation if left for more than a few days with no sugar, so it's important to make new batches on a regular schedule. Fortunately, once you taste your water kefir, you'll want to make it all the time!

Dissolve the sugar in a half gallon (2 L) Mason jar containing 1 quart (1 L) of water. Or to speed the process, dissolve the sugar in the jar with 1 cup (250 ml) hot water and then add 3 cups (750 ml) cold water to get to a total of 1 quart (1 L). Make sure that the resulting sugar-water mixture is body temperature (98°F or 37°C) or lower.

Add the kefir grains and the eggshell, raisins, or aguamiel de maguey (if using) and then cover with a lid. Write the brewing date on a piece of masking tape on the outside of the jar.

Let it sit at room temperature for 24 to 48 hours until you see bubbling activity.

As with Milk Kefir (see page 88), strain the kefir grains with a plastic or nylon strainer and start a new batch immediately, if possible.

Refrigerate the fermented water kefir liquid in a covered jar until ready to serve.

For a different flavor, perform a second fermentation: In a half gallon (2 L) Mason jar, add some chopped fruit to the brewed water kefir. Close the lid. Write the brewing date on a piece of masking tape on the outside of the jar.

Let it sit at room temperature for another 24 to 48 hours, at which time it will be ready to drink or to refrigerate.

Be careful when opening the kefir; it has more fizz than kombucha and can explode. It's a good idea to refrigerate the bottle one or two hours before opening it. This will lessen the explosion potential. Once opened, strain the fruit, if desired, and serve.

KOMBUCHA AND JUN

Kombucha is a sweet and sour fermented tea drink and health tonic that probably originated in Central Asia centuries ago. It is the product of a bacteria- and-yeast fermentation with a base of sweetened tea. Today, kombucha is generally made with refined cane sugar (table sugar or granulated sugar), although in the past it would have been made with whatever sweetener was available. Most of the sugar introduced while making kombucha is metabolized by the microbes during fermentation.

KOMBUCHA, METHOD 1: BATCH 105

KOMBUCHA, METHOD 2: CONTINUOUS-BREW 108

SCOBY FROM STORE- BOUGHT KOMBUCHA 111

FLAVORED KOMBUCHA: SECOND FERMENTATION (2F) 112

COFFEE KOMBUCHA 113

JUN 114

It is possible that, like many fermented foods, kombucha was first created by accident. It's easy to imagine people making sweetened tea, drinking most of it, and pouring the leftover into a vat—and then discovering that the contents of the vat had an intriguing smell. Perhaps some brave soul tasted it, or perhaps someone mistook it for sour wine vinegar. Perhaps someone who was already making fruit vinegar decided to try adding some sweet tea to it, and then they started using more tea and less fruit. In any case, the yeasts and bacteria that make up the kombucha culture likely found their home serendipitously.

Just what exactly are those yeasts and bacteria? It depends. Like yogurt, cheese, and many other fermented foods, kombucha is not the product of one specific, fixed, globally constant menagerie of microbes, in precise ratios—it's a descriptive label fitting a category of foods with similar characteristics.

Jun is kombucha's shy cousin, made with not just any sweetener but with honey specifically. In fact, jun may predate sugarcane-based kombucha; honey was widespread before sugarcane was. The distinction between kombucha and jun is slightly arbitrary, as kombucha can be made

THE MANY NAMES OF KOMBUCHA

Hannah Crum, "The Kombucha Mamma," lists the many names of Kombucha:

- Champagne of Life
- Champignon de Longue Vie
- Combucha
- The Divine Tsche
- Embuya Orientalis
- Fungus Japonicus
- Gout Jelly-fish
- Hongo
- Indian Tea Fungus
- Japanese Tea Fungus
- Kambotscha
- Kargasok tea
- Kombucha Fungus

- Koucha kinoko
- Kwassan
- Manchu Fungus
- Manchurian Mushroom
- Manchurian Tea
- Miracle Fungus
- Mo-Gu
- Mother of Vinegar
- Mushroom of Charity
- Olinka
- Pinchia Fermentans
- The Remedy of Immortality
- Russian Jelly-fish

- Russian Tea-vinegar
- Spumonto
- T'chai from the Sea
- The Tea Beast
- Tea beer
- Tea Cider
- Tea Kvass
- Tea Mould
- Tea Mushroom
- Teepilz
- Teekwass Fungus
- Tschambucco
- Volga Fungus

with sweeteners or combinations of sweeteners beyond just cane sugar. If you make it with half sugar and half honey, is it kombucha or jun?

Some of the notable differences between kombucha and jun arise because kombucha is brewed from a disaccharide, and jun is brewed from a monosaccharide. (See chapter 3 on page 34.) This means that (a) jun generally brews more quickly than kombucha and (b) jun may be a better choice for people following the GAPS diet or for people with profound gut issues. Jun also seems to be a bit more temperamental with respect to brewing.

Kombucha and jun have both spread far and wide, finding homes among diverse groups of health-conscious people. Consider the many names in many languages that kombucha has received over the years!

THE RISE OF KOMBUCHA

Kombucha stepped into the Western mainstream in the 1990s with a couple of important milestones. One was the publication of Günther Frank's monograph, *Kombucha: Healthy Beverage and Natural Remedy from the Far East, Its Correct Preparation and Use*, which has since been translated into many languages. It was also around this time that some Americans with AIDS and cancer took interest in kombucha as a possible immune-system booster.

Riding the rising tide of kombucha, the *New York Times* in 1994 published a playfully sensationalist article with a controversial-sounding title: "A Magic Mushroom or a Toxic Fad?" The article discussed kombucha's perceived potential danger, the culture getting contaminated in some unspecified way, although it gave no examples of contamination happening and mentioned that the FDA had not received any reports of adverse reactions to it. The article mostly dismissed the safety concerns, although it also mostly dismissed the potential benefits. Regardless, it brought more public attention to kombucha, documented its public perception, and yielded some excellent quotes, including, ". . . Kombucha is the pet rock of the 90's— except that it is alive."

Among those who became interested in kombucha for its immune-boosting properties was a Los Angeles native named GT Dave, whose mother Laraine had been diagnosed with cancer. She credits kombucha for helping her through cancer. In her words (as explained in her testimony on Synergydrinks.com), "I credit kombucha for keeping me strong, before, during, and after my cancer treatment." The family now runs GT's Kombucha, the world's biggest kombucha business. In 1999, early in its existence, GT's Kombucha became available for purchase at Whole Foods, the high-end American natural grocery chain. GT's grew quickly from there.

Today, the kombucha business in the United States alone is many hundreds of millions of dollars per year. Its producers even have their own trade organization, Kombucha Brewers International, founded by kombucha advocates and entrepreneurs Hannah Crum and Alex

LaGory. It's safe to say that kombucha is no longer exotic, obscure, or even scarce in much of the United States. And it continues to grow in popularity.

WHY HOMEBREW?

But kombucha is still not universal, especially outside the United States. Because it's a live, fermenting drink, it requires consistent refrigeration, making it more difficult to transport and distribute than soda, its nominal competitor. In poorer countries, the refrigerated supply chain, which is responsible for distributing refrigerated products such as milk, is not as reliable as in rich countries. And in some countries—such as Singapore—commercial sale of kombucha has been entirely banned due to perceived safety concerns.

Fortunately, if you want to drink kombucha but are unable to find it in stores, you can make it yourself. (Or perhaps you can find someone to sell it to you privately—there's a kombucha underground on the Internet!) You can also save money making it yourself. Buying organic kombucha in the store can cost $3 to $5 per pint (500 ml) in the United States, sometimes more; making it costs about a tenth of that using comparable ingredients (organic tea, organic sugar, and filtered water).

Yet another reason to make it yourself is formulation. In 2010, a United States government agency tested bottles of kombucha taken from supermarket shelves and found that some exceeded the 0.5% ABV (alcohol by volume) allowed for "non-alcoholic" beverages. (See "Measuring Alcohol" on page 184 for information on ABV.) These bottles may not have been properly refrigerated during distribution; improper handling can increase alcohol concentration. There are also questions about the accuracy of the outdated methods used by the government to assess ABV. Regardless, kombucha makers were forced to either reformulate their brews to prevent alcohol buildup, or sell them as alcoholic beverages. GT's Kombucha has done both, offering two lines of kombucha: Enlightened (reformulated) and Classic (original). Reformulated kombucha contains a different balance of microbes from kombucha's historic balance and has a hard time perpetuating itself when used as a starter. If you want a traditional pre-twenty-first century kombucha with all the traditional probiotic benefits, you might consider brewing your own kombucha.

At least one company, Dr. Hops Kombucha Beer, has taken a different tack. They are creating a line of high-alcohol kombuchas, between 5% and 10% ABV, with the express intent of distributing and selling them as alcoholic beverages. It seems like a good strategy; cocktail aficionados are always looking for something new. For what it's worth, it's not clear that all of kombucha's health benefits persist at these alcohol levels. Some of the microbes may not survive, and some of the enzymes will probably be denatured, but the vitamins and minerals should do fine.

WHAT YOU'LL NEED

You need three things to brew kombucha: sugar; plain tea from the tea plant *Camellia sinensis*; and some amount of live kombucha, preferably including a piece of SCOBY mat.

SUGAR

Cane sugar, ideally organic, is the easiest sugar to use. Beet sugar is not recommended because it is almost always genetically modified. For more on sugars and sweeteners, see page 63.

TEA

Black tea, oolong tea, and green tea all come from the plant *Camellia sinensis*, and they are your best options for brewing kombucha. Many of the other things commonly called "tea" are flavored teas, herbal infusions, or something else. Mint tea, chamomile tea, and rooibos, for example, are herbal infusions. Earl Grey is a black tea flavored with oil of bergamot; oils and bergamot can inhibit fermentation, so Earl Grey is not a good choice for making kombucha.

Compounds in *Camellia sinensis* are key to the longevity of the kombucha culture. If you use plain tea from *Camellia sinensis*, you should be able to continue your kombucha brewing indefinitely, for as many generations as you like. You may be able to make kombucha with other flavorful sweetened liquids for a few generations, but these kombucha lineages will likely fail sooner or later. Even combinations of *Camellia*

103

sinensis and herbs may not work in the long run. Our best advice is to brew with plain tea and then add any other flavorings while bottling, followed by some more time at room temperature. This way, your brewing remains as simple and reliable as possible, and the challenges to your SCOBY are minimized.

That said, when you do find yourself with surplus kombucha SCOBYs, you can attempt interesting kombucha variants by brewing with rooibos, yerba mate, coffee, or something else. Some adventurers have even made kombucha out of unlikely sounding sweet beverages such as orange soda. Experimentation is great; just

A WORD ON WATER

Use filtered water when brewing your tea for kombucha because municipal water supplies often have added chlorine, and chlorine is antimicrobial. (For more on water, see page 61.) Boiling tap water for 30 minutes and allowing it to cool may remove some types of chlorination; if you boil your water but find yourself having ongoing problems with your ferments, try using a water filter or bottled water. Once you start investing more time in fermentation, the expense of a water filter is easy to justify—it's cheap fermenting insurance, not to mention a wise investment in healthier drinking water!

don't be surprised if these kombucha lineages die out. If you want to stay in the game in the long term, keep around some SCOBYs that have seen only tea and sugar.

SCOBY

When discussing kombucha, you've probably encountered the term SCOBY, an acronym for Symbiotic Community of Bacteria and Yeast. So what is it? To be precise, a kombucha SCOBY is a collection of kombucha microbes that is used to brew, or ferment, each batch. (Technically you can have a *kefir SCOBY* or *vinegar SCOBY* as well, since these both involve SCOBYs to culture or ferment the liquid, but in practice, the term *SCOBY* is not used much beyond kombucha and its cousin jun.) The most visible aspect of the SCOBY, also called the mother, is an off-white mat that looks like a slimy Frisbee or a calamari steak. This mat floats on top of a fermenting batch of kombucha, providing a convenient residence for some of the bacteria and yeast—like a coral reef for microbes. The mat is a by-product of the fermentation and is not the be-all and end-all of kombucha brewing; it may receive more attention than it deserves. That said, the growth of the mat is excellent evidence of the activity and viability of a batch of kombucha. And the growth of the mat regulates the liquid's access to oxygen; oxygen restriction will favor anaerobic fermentation and may affect the composition and progression of kombucha in crucial ways.

We'll use the term *SCOBY* to refer specifically to the mat.

104

KOMBUCHA
METHOD I: BATCH

The batch method is ideal for first-time kombucha brewers, as it allows you to bottle and refresh a new batch of kombucha each week, in moderate proportions (which you can increase and decrease as you see fit). It's also the best method for experimental kombuchas, such as that coffee kombucha or rooibos kombucha you're dying to try, where the brew may not propagate beyond a few generations. Some people prefer the batch method regardless.

YIELD: I QUART (I L)

1 quart (1 L) filtered water

1 tablespoon (5 g) loose-leaf tea, or 2 tea bags

¼ cup (50 g) sugar

¼ cup (60 ml) mature kombucha liquid

1 healthy kombucha SCOBY (may be small; see page 111 for information about how to get one)

Boil 1 pint (500 ml) of water in a small pot over high heat. Remove from the heat, add the tea, and let steep for at least 5 minutes.

Remove the tea leaves or bags. Add the sugar and stir with a wooden spoon until dissolved. Add the remaining 1 pint (500 ml) of room temperature water.

Once the sweetened tea has cooled to body temperature or below, transfer to a large glass jar with a wide mouth, leaving at least 3 inches (8 cm) of space on top. Add the kombucha liquid and place the SCOBY on top of the liquid (if it sinks, that's okay). Cover the jar with a clean cloth, kitchen towel, paper towel, or coffee filter and secure it with a rubber band. Write the brewing date on a piece of masking tape and stick it to the outside of the jar.

Let it sit at warm room temperature, between 75°F and 85°F (24°C and 30°C), if practical. How long your kombucha needs to brew depends on

105

ambient temperature. It can take 5 days in warm weather or 2 to 4 weeks when it's cold. (There are ways to accelerate brewing under colder conditions by keeping your kombucha warm. Generally, they involve using a heater or insulation. If you have a cold stone countertop, try putting a mat under your brewing vessel.)

During the brewing, a new SCOBY may form on top of the jar, above the old SCOBY. Once a reasonably thick new SCOBY has formed to cover the top part of the liquid, the kombucha is well on its way to being ready. Taste it, using a clean ladle; it should be tart. If it's still too sweet, wait another day or two and taste it again.

Some people, including many new kombucha enthusiasts, will prefer a sweeter, milder kombucha. Long time kombucha consumers usually ferment it longer for a stronger, more acidic taste. There is a direct inverse relation between sugar content (sweetness) and acid content (sourness/strong flavor) because sugar is transformed into acid by fermentation. The longer the fermentation, the sourer the batch.

Once the kombucha has reached the desired flavor, put the SCOBY aside with a bit of the liquid. Pour the finished kombucha through a strainer and bottle it in glass bottles, Mason jars, or BPA-free plastic bottles. Cap it, optionally leave it out a day or two if you want effervescence, and refrigerate it. (See page 55 for a longer discussion of bottling and page 112 for a discussion of secondary fermentation.)

To make a new batch of kombucha, repeat the same process using your SCOBY and reserved liquid as a starter. If you don't want to start a new batch immediately, don't strain off and bottle the liquid—just leave it as is. The kombucha will become more and more vinegary. It can be left this way for a couple of months, depending on temperature and other conditions—just make sure to top it off with sweet tea if the liquid level gets too low. When you are ready to start a new batch of kombucha, strain off the kombucha vinegar, use it as you would use any other vinegar, and start from the top. (Using vinegary kombucha as the starter for a new batch is fine.)

KOMBUCHA
METHOD 2: CONTINUOUS-BREW

Here's the exact continuous-brew kombucha setup that Alex has been using on and off for some years. It yields roughly a gallon (4 L) of drinkable kombucha per week during the summer and fall (even in cold San Francisco!) and half that during the winter. If that's not enough for your needs, you can either double (or triple, or whatever) all the amounts and sizes, or you can run multiple brews in parallel. One deciding factor may be weight. Will you need to move your brewing setup? Glass vessels are heavy, as is kombucha (water weighs 8 pounds per gallon, or 4 kilograms per 4 liters)! Another deciding factor may be your willingness to spend money on a large vessel—they can be expensive. You can also use a pre-configured continuous brew setup; kombuchakamp.com and other sites sell these. (See "Resources" on page 200 for more information.)

YIELD: 8 TO 16 OUNCES (250 TO 500 ML) KOMBUCHA PER DAY, DEPENDING ON AMBIENT TEMPERATURE

BASIC EQUIPMENT

1 two gallon (8 L), open-topped glass cookie jar with a bung hole near the bottom

The advantages of the continuous-brew method include the following:

- Because you are never starting from scratch, there is a more consistently low pH during brewing, decreasing the likelihood of contamination.

- There is less pouring of sticky liquids back and forth.

1 polypropylene, BPA-free, acid-safe, made-in-USA (to ensure the material meets safety standards) spigot to fit cookie jar (with gaskets as needed)

1 half gallon (2 L) Mason jar

1 clean kitchen towel

1 large rubber band

ADDITIONAL EQUIPMENT

1 long-handled wooden spoon

1 electronic scale
(with at least 1 g resolution)

If using loose tea: 1 more half gallon (2 L) Mason jar, and a fine-mesh strainer

BOTTLING EQUIPMENT

1 or more half gallon (2 L) carboys

OR at least two quarts' (2 L) worth of Mason jars of any size

OR at least 4 old commercial 16 ounce (500 ml) kombucha bottles

STARTER INGREDIENTS

1 healthy kombucha SCOBY

1 to 4 quarts (1 to 4 L) kombucha liquid

REFRESH INGREDIENTS

130 grams (approximately $2/3$ cup) granulated sugar

2 quarts (2 L) water

10 grams organic tea (approximately 5 teaspoons, or 4 tea bags—2 black and 2 green)

- Scheduling flexibility is somewhat increased.

- You may encounter a more diverse menagerie of microbes because more phases of the kombucha metabolism take place simultaneously.

The downsides are as follows:

- There is a somewhat greater up-front investment in equipment.

- There is more of a need for a permanent location for the equipment because it may be bigger and heavier.

METHOD

Once things are up and running, the goal is to maintain 6 quarts (6 L) of liquid in the brewing vessel, with a SCOBY on top. From time to time, we drain off 2 quarts (2 L) of fully-brewed kombucha via the spigot and bottle it; then we add 2 quarts (2 L) of brewed sweet tea back to the brewing vessel to bring the total amount back up to 6 quarts (6 L). Then we let the kombucha brew for some number of days, until it's done; then we bottle another 2 quarts (2 L) of fully brewed kombucha as before and repeat. In a warm environment, the entire cycle might take as little as 3 days; in a colder environment, it could take 8 days.

The SCOBY at the top of the jar will become thicker and gain layers as time goes on. When it gets more than 1 to 2 inches (2.5 to 5 cm) thick, peel off several layers by hand and give them, along with some liquid, to a friend, so that your friend can start making kombucha! Or give them to a stranger via craigslist, reddit, or Facebook. Grind them up and use them as a facial mask, or feed them to your dog or goat. Folks have even dried them and sewn them into SCOBY-leather jackets!

INITIAL SETUP

If you have a glass jar with a plastic or metallic spigot, remove the spigot because it is unlikely that it is suitable for long-term use in an acidic environment. Install the new spigot that you bought separately and ensure that it has a good, watertight seal by putting some water in the jar and checking for leaks. It's best to sort this out now, when there's no kombucha in the jar!

Pour 6 quarts (6 L) water into the jar. (You can use the half gallon [2 L] Mason jar as a measuring cup.) Place a piece of masking tape on the side of the jar so that the top of the tape is at the level of 6 quarts (6 L) of water in the jar. Dump out the water, but leave the tape on the jar.

Place the SCOBY and initial kombucha in the jar. Arrange a clean kitchen towel over the top of the vessel and secure it with a rubber band.

Brew sweet tea using the procedure below, and add it to the jar until SCOBY and tea reach the tape mark.

CONTINUOUS BREWING

Place the tea bags or loose tea in a half gallon [2 L] Mason jar. Boil 1 quart (1 L) of water and pour into the Mason jar over the tea. Let steep for 15 minutes. Remove the tea bags, or if you are using loose tea, pour the liquid through a strainer into another Mason jar. Stir the sugar into the tea with a wooden spoon until dissolved. Add 1 more quart (1 L) of room temperature water.

At this point, the sweetened tea should not be so hot that it burns your finger. Stick your (clean!) index finger into the brewed, sweetened tea and leave it there for a count of ten. If it hurts, the tea is too hot; let it cool and try again later. Once the tea is cool enough for your finger, it's cool enough for the kombucha.

Remove the rubber band and the kitchen towel from the top of your kombucha vessel.

If the kombucha liquid in the jar is at or above the level of the tape, give it a vigorous stir with the wooden spoon to distribute the sediment and yeast evenly in the vessel. (Don't worry if this disturbs the SCOBY floating at the top of the liquid.) Drain off liquid via the spigot into a glass until the level of the liquid matches the tape. Drink it or save it for bottling. Drain off a further half gallon (2 L) of the liquid via the spigot into your bottling containers.

Pour the tea into the brewing vessel over the SCOBY. The level of the liquid should be close to the tape. If the liquid is a little below the tape, add filtered water until they align. Give it a stir.

Replace the kitchen towel and rubber band.

After 3 days, drain off some liquid via the spigot into a small glass and taste it. If it's too sweet, wait another day or two and try again before bottling your 2 quarts (2 L) or so. Be prepared to try a few times if your brewing environment is on the colder side. Once it tastes right, repeat the entire procedure, from the top!

SCOBY
FROM STORE-BOUGHT KOMBUCHA

If you don't have a SCOBY available, you *may* be able to grow one from a bottle of store-bought kombucha. If you are in the United States, you will have the best chances of success with a classic-style kombucha rather than a reformulated one (see page 102). Classic kombuchas are typically labeled and sold as alcoholic beverages, although their alcohol content is generally quite low.

YIELD: 1 SCOBY

2 cups (500 ml) filtered water

$\frac{1}{2}$ tablespoon (5 g) loose-tea leaves, or 1 tea bag

2 tablespoons (25 g) granulated sugar

1 bottle (12 to 16 ounces, or 375 to 500 ml) store-bought, raw, unflavored, tea-based kombucha

Boil 2 cups (500 ml) of water in a small pot over high heat. Remove from the heat, add the tea, and let steep for 5 to 10 minutes. Remove the tea leaves and add the sugar; stir until dissolved. Let cool until comfortable to the touch.

Transfer the tea to a half gallon (2 L) Mason jar and pour in the store-bought kombucha. Cover with a clean cloth, kitchen towel, paper towel, or coffee filter and secure it with a rubber band or Mason jar ring. Leave it at room temperature.

Depending mostly on temperature, a SCOBY may form in 1 to 3 weeks. Be patient, but if nothing has happened after 6 weeks, it's likely that nothing will happen—it's time to give up and try again.

Let the SCOBY thicken to $\frac{1}{4}$ inch (6 mm) if it's growing—but it's probably okay if it doesn't get to that thickness. Use it to make your next batch of kombucha!

FLAVORED KOMBUCHA
SECOND FERMENTATION (2F)

Secondary fermentation is a nice way to give kombucha a kick. It can make it more bubbly and impart some interesting flavors. (See sidebar). If flavoring larger batches of kombucha, increase the amount of fruit you use accordingly. Flip-top (Grolsch-style) bottles work well, as do commercial kombucha bottles, Mason jars, or small carboys or growlers.

Up to ¼ cup (55 g) fresh, dried, or frozen fruit per quart (liter) kombucha

Fresh or dried herbs, spices, and roots to taste

16 ounces (500 ml) or more kombucha

Peel any nonorganic ingredients. Cut or chop everything into small pieces or purée in a food processor.

Pour the kombucha liquid (without the SCOBY) into bottles, leaving space for the ingredients you will be adding. Add the fruit and other ingredients, leaving as little air as possible. Seal or cap tightly. Write the brewing date

SUGGESTED FLAVOR COMBINATIONS

Here are some of our favorite fruit and spice/herb combos for flavor-based kombucha:

- Blueberry Lavender
- Guava Rose
- Turmeric Raisin
- Grapefruit Rosemary

- Strawberry Mint
- Cherry Basil
- Orange Ginger
- Mixed Berry

- Rose Tea Cherry
- Ginger Lemon

on pieces of masking tape and stick them to the outside of the bottles.

Let them sit at room temperature for 2 days to 2 weeks. The warmer it is, the less time is needed.

To prevent kombucha explosions, refrigerate the bottles of kombucha for at least 1 hour before opening. Serve as is or strain out any solids before drinking. Refrigerate after opening.

BOTTLING TIP: Bottle some of your kombucha in a small, BPA-free plastic bottle. Squeeze the bottle during the secondary fermentation process to get a sense of how much pressure has built up. For a further discussion of bottling strategies, see page 55.

WARNING: Do not shake before opening. It can create quite a mess! Swirling gently is okay.

COFFEE KOMBUCHA

Here's another way to get a different flavor: Use a different liquid . . . such as coffee! The new SCOBY this batch forms may or may not be healthy enough to create another batch. To maximize your chances of success, use a tea-bred SCOBY for every new batch of coffee kombucha you make.

YIELD: I QUART (I L), ABOUT 3 TO 4 SERVINGS

¼ cup (50 g) granulated sugar

1 quart (1 L) freshly brewed coffee

Kombucha SCOBY

¼ cup (60 ml) kombucha liquid

Dissolve the sugar in the hot coffee in a half gallon (2 L) Mason jar and let it cool to room temperature. Add the SCOBY and kombucha liquid. Cover with a clean cloth, kitchen towel, paper towel, or coffee filter and secure it with rubber band or Mason jar ring. Write the brewing date on a piece of masking tape and stick it to the outside of the jar.

Leave it at room temperature approximately 7 days or until a new kombucha SCOBY has formed.

113

JUN

Jun is a kombucha variant made with honey as the sweetener. There are a few notable differences between the two:

- Jun brews quicker than sugar kombucha, perhaps because (disaccharide) sugar used for kombucha needs to be broken down into its constituent fructose and glucose, whereas (mostly monosaccharide) honey used for jun does not need this breakdown process.
- Jun is happier brewing at lower temperatures than kombucha.
- Jun does best with green tea, while kombucha brewed with sugar seems to be less picky.
- Because honey has already been broken down into fructose and glucose, it is suitable for people on the GAPS diet, while sugar (sucrose) is not.

So brewing jun rather than standard kombucha might make sense if you have a steady source of honey, if you live in a cooler climate, or if you have a health reason to favor it. On the other hand, if you buy your sweeteners at the store, brewing standard kombucha will be significantly cheaper than brewing jun because sugar is cheaper than honey.

This recipe is just like the batch kombucha recipe on page 105, except that instead of dissolving sugar in hot tea, we dissolve honey in somewhat cooler tea. This preserves the enzymes in the raw honey.

YIELD: 4 SERVINGS

1 quart (1 L) filtered water

1 tablespoon green
tea leaves (5 g)
or 2 bags green tea

¼ cup (75 g) raw honey

½ cup (125 ml) liquid Jun

1 healthy Jun SCOBY

Boil 1 pint (500 ml) of water in a small pot over high heat. Remove from the heat, add the tea, and let steep for at least 5 minutes.

Remove the tea leaves. Add the remaining 1 pint (500 ml) of room temperature water. Test the water temperature with your finger. When it's comfortable to your finger, add the honey and stir with a wooden spoon until dissolved.

Transfer to a large glass jar with a wide mouth, leaving at least 3 inches (8 cm) of space on top. Add the jun liquid and place the SCOBY on top. Cover with a clean cloth, kitchen towel, paper towel, or coffee filter and secure it with a rubber band. Write the brewing date on a piece of masking tape on the outside of the jar.

Let it sit at room temperature, between 68°F and 77°F (20°C and 25°C), if practical. How long your jun needs to brew depends on ambient temperature, but it usually brews quicker than kombucha. Three to 5 days is a good window.

During the brewing, a new SCOBY may form on top of the jar and the old SCOBY may sink. Once a reasonably thick new SCOBY has formed to cover the top part of the liquid, the jun is well on its way to being ready. Taste it, using a clean ladle; it should be tart. If it's still too sweet, wait another day or two and taste it again.

Proceed as for Kombucha on page 105.

Alternately, use the continuous-brew method by following the steps on page 108. Replace the kombucha SCOBY, liquid, and sugar with the jun SCOBY, liquid, and honey. Remember that jun brews best in green tea.

VEGETABLE DRINKS

Fermented vegetable drinks have more B and C vitamins than their fresh juice cousins. Because of the fermentation, they also contain significantly more enzymes and less sugar, since the microbes produce enzymes to transform sugars into acids, vitamins, and other things. The sugar in fresh juices can be problematic for some people. And these are just the advantages that fermented juices have over fresh, raw juices. When you look at commercial pasteurized juices, even 100% juice, not from concentrate juices, or cold pasteurized juices, the differences are even more dramatic because the enzymes and some vitamins are lost in processing.

BEET KVASS 118

CUCUMBER PICKLE BRINE 120

RADISH BRINE 122

JUICED FERMENTED VEGETABLES 123

KIMCHI SODA 124

FERMENTED GREEN JUICE 125

BEET KVASS

Beet kvass is the brine from fermented beets (beetroot). It combines the benefits of beets with the benefits of fermentation! Beets contain vitamin B$_9$ (folate) and vitamin C, plus iron and a variety of minerals that are necessary for proper nerve and muscle function and for healthy bones, liver, kidneys, and pancreas.

Beet kvass is easy to make, and a shot of it is a great morning tonic and organ cleanser. If you buy organic beets and ginger, you don't even have to peel them. This recipe works well in a half gallon (2 L) Mason jar.

YIELD: ABOUT 1½ QUARTS (1.5 L)

2 or 3 beets, peeled if not organic

1 inch (2.5 cm) of fresh ginger, peeled if not organic (optional)

1 inch (2.5 cm) of sprig rosemary (optional)

Approximately 1½ quarts (1.5 L) filtered water

1 tablespoon (15 g) sea salt

Coarsely chop the beets into ½- to 1-inch (1 to 2.5 cm) pieces. Cut the ginger (if using) into ¼-inch (6 mm) chunks. Place the beets, ginger, and rosemary (if using) in a half gallon (2 L) Mason jar. Fill the jar halfway with filtered water. Add the salt, close the lid, and shake. Once the salt has dissolved, open the lid and fill with water to the shoulder of the jar, leaving 1 to 2 inches (2.5 to 5 cm) of space at the top. Close the lid. Write the date on a piece of masking tape and stick it to the outside of the jar.

Let it sit for a few days to 1 week if your room is warm, or for 2 or 3 weeks if it's cooler. The kvass will progress well if you keep the lid closed. Gently agitate once a day to ensure that mold does not form. You know it's on its way when it starts getting foamy. Once you open the lid, though, it's best to strain the kvass and refrigerate it because if you close it again and leave it at room temperature, molds can take hold.

When you're ready to put it into the fridge, pour it through a strainer to separate the beets (and other optional ingredients) from the liquid. The kvass is the liquid. Keep it covered in the refrigerator and drink it cold if you like.

Keep the beet chunks in the refrigerator, too. They can be chopped up and thrown in salads or soups, blended and added to salad dressing, or put through a juicer. Or you can blend the beet chunks with some of the kvass as the base for a fermented beet gazpacho or borscht!

VARIATION: Substitute 6 carrots for the beets. (Ginger goes well in carrot kvass; rosemary may overwhelm it.) Carrot kvass is a good option for people who don't like beets, and it's a good way to start developing a taste for fermented tonics.

CUCUMBER PICKLE BRINE

This is a fermented pickle recipe that is quicker than some, and it produces a nice brine. If you run into mold problems, add more leaves or spices and/or bump up the amount of salt a bit. Oak, grape, and mesquite leaves, tea, and pickling spices all contain tannins. Tannins are anti-fungal, so they discourage molds and yeasts from populating the pickles and pickle brine. Garlic and ginger have antifungal properties too.

YIELD: ABOUT 1 QUART (1 L) OF BRINE

2½ tablespoons (40 g) sea salt

1 quart (1 L) filtered water

1 to 2 cups (125 to 250 g) coarsely chopped cucumber

Your choice of herbs and spices such as peeled whole cloves garlic, peeled (if not organic) and sliced ginger, sliced or rough-cut onions or small pearl onions, pickling spices, and/or whole peppercorns

1 or 2 oak, grape, or mesquite leaves, or one black tea bag

Prepare the brine: Stir the salt into the filtered water in a wide mouth Mason jar or a ceramic crock until dissolved. If you are impatient, heat some of the water, dissolve the salt in it, and then add the rest of the cooler water; be sure that the liquid is approximately room temperature before proceeding.

Place the cucumbers, herbs, spices, and leaves into a jar. Pour the brine over the vegetables, covering them by at least 2 inches (5 cm). Weighing down the vegetables to keep them under the brine is helpful, although it is not strictly necessary. This can be accomplished with a small plate; ceramic fermentation weights; boiled large, flat stones; or other vegetable pieces and can help prevent mold from becoming a problem and keep things crisper.

Close the lid and place the jar on top of a tray in case it leaks. This is a good opportunity to use a jar-size airlock, if you have one. (See chapter 4 on page 46.) Write the date on a piece of masking tape and stick it to the outside of the jar.

If you're not using an airlock, then during the first few days, pressure will build up. It is a good idea to check the jar once or twice a day. Burp the jar by quickly opening and closing the lid to let pressure out.

Taste on day 3. Once the pickles have softened a little and the brine tastes like pickles, transfer to the refrigerator. You can eat the pickles and drink the brine at any time.

Don't let the cucumbers ferment for too long during hot weather because they can quickly become soft or develop mold. If you see mold forming on top, discard and start again. Even if the pickles don't get moldy, they can lose their crispness. Soft pickles aren't much fun, but even if you throw out the pickles, if there are no signs of mold, the brine is a great probiotic drink.

RADISH BRINE

Radish brine is a twist on a regular pickle brine, with an intense, peppery flavor.

Up to 1 cup (75 g) finely shredded cabbage (optional)

2½ tablespoons (40 g) plus 1 teaspoon (5 g) sea salt

1 quart (1 L) filtered water

1 to 2 cups (125 to 225 g) whole or halved radishes

Your choice of herbs and spices such as peeled whole or sliced garlic; peeled (if not organic) and sliced ginger; small onions; and/ or pickling spices, such as bay leaves, oak leaves, cinnamon, mustard seeds, whole peppercorns

Place the cabbage (if using) in a large mixing bowl. Add 1 teaspoon (5 g) of salt and mix thoroughly with your clean hands. Squeeze until the shredded cabbage releases its juice.

Prepare the brine: Stir 2½ tablespoons (40 g) of salt into the filtered water in a wide mouth jar or mixing bowl until dissolved.

Place the radishes and spices in a large jar. Add the cabbage and its juice. Pour the brine over the vegetables, covering them by at least 2 inches (5 cm). Weigh down the vegetables with something to keep them below the surface, if desired. Depending on what vessel you're using, weight options include a small plate, ceramic fermentation weights, and other vegetable pieces.

Close the lid and place the jar on top of a tray. Write the date on a piece of masking tape and stick it to the outside of the jar.

During the first few days, pressure will build up. It is a good idea to check the jar once or twice a day. Burp the jar by quickly opening and closing the lid to let pressure out. Or if you prefer, use an airlock lid. (See chapter 4 on page 46.)

Start tasting around day 5. Once you like the taste, transfer to the refrigerator or leave at room temperature.

JUICED FERMENTED VEGETABLES

Fermented vegetables such as sauerkraut and kimchi can be easily transformed into a probiotic drink or tonic. Put your fermented vegetables through a juicer and *voilá*! You can drink the liquid straight out of the juicer. Or you may want to enjoy it gradually, by bottling it and refrigerating it. Serve it with raw oysters or clams as a shooter or in a shot glass as a digestif chaser for a cheese and charcuterie plate.

If you have jars of vegetable ferments that have been sitting in your fridge staring at you for longer than you'd care to admit, this is a great

destiny for them. It's also good for mixology—folks are always looking for cocktail inspiration. You can mix it with beer to make a fermented michelada or with vodka as part of a fermented Kimchi Bloody Mary (see page 193).

For how to make fermented vegetables beyond the cucumber pickles and radishes, see the "Resources" section, search the Internet, or check out Alex's previous book, *Real Food Fermentation*.

KIMCHI SODA

Who can resist kimchi soda?! It's spicy, garlicky, and briny. A salt rim is a possibility, but probably redundant! If you need something to wake you up in the morning, take a good chug of kimchi soda. You may not need coffee anymore. And all that garlic may keep the mosquitos away, not to mention your coworkers, family, and friends!

YIELD: 2 SERVINGS

½ cup (75 g) kimchi

2 cups (500 ml) sparkling water

A dash of lime (optional)

Ice (optional)

Put the kimchi through a juicer or blend it in a blender and strain the juice. Pour the kimchi juice into two glasses to serve. Try margarita or beer glasses if you want to explore a salt rim or champagne glasses to show off the bubbles. Add sparkling water, lime, and ice (if using) and serve. If you're a real kimchi lover, add more kimchi juice or even garnish with chunks or slices of kimchi.

FERMENTED GREEN JUICE

Our friend Marcela Merino, raw food chef and founder of *Rawdelicious*, gave us this recipe. She always has amazing recipes for green juices and smoothies, so we thought it would be fun to try a fermentation twist on one of her basic green juices. Try it with a salt rim!

YIELD: I SERVING

½ of a cucumber, peeled

4 celery sticks

1 cup fresh or fermented (30 g or 180 g) spinach or (70 g or 130 g) kale

1 green apple

1 lemon, peeled (if not organic) and quartered

1 inch (2.5 cm) ginger, peeled if not organic

¼ cup (40 g) sauerkraut

Put all the ingredients through a juicer. Serve immediately.

125

SODAS

A soda is any type of sweet drink with bubbles that is not alcoholic or has only trace amounts of alcohol. When we think about sodas, we usually picture a Coca-Cola or a Mountain Dew. But this is not the picture of a healthy probiotic drink!

The Kimchi Soda recipe on page 124 was not an anomaly; in this chapter, we will show you that making delicious sodas at home is easy, cheap, and healthy. Adding fermented sodas to your diet is a great way to curb your consumption of unhealthy sodas. Even your kids will love them!

HIBISCUS SODA   128

GRAPE SODA   130

FRUITY SODA   131

LEMONGINA/LIMEGINA   132

ORANGINA   134

FRUIT JUICE SODAS   135

COCONUT SODA KEFIR   136

HIBISCUS SODA

Jamaica is the Mexican name for hibiscus. It is also the name of one of the most popular and widely consumed homemade drinks in Mexico; it's made from water, hibiscus flower, and sugar. When you sit down to lunch at a Mexican home, you may be asked: *"Limonada* or *Jamaica?"* As a kid, Raquel never thought Jamaica was anything other than a red, sweet, delicious, and refreshing drink.

About a year ago, Raquel invited Sandor Katz to her hometown of Monterrey, Mexico, where he led a fermentation conference. One day while they were discussing the differences between kombucha and other fermented beverages, she asked him how to introduce kombucha into her community. With a mischievous smile, he suggested, "Why don't you start by wildly fermenting a beverage that everybody already likes and is used to?" Thus, Hibiscus Soda was born—a wild fermentation recipe—ambient microbes do the work, and no starter is needed.

**YIELD: ABOUT
6 SERVINGS (8 OUNCES,
OR 250 ML, EACH**

8 cups (2 L) filtered water

2½ ounces (75 g) dried
hibiscus flowers

¾ cup (150 g) granulated sugar

Bring the water to a boil in a saucepan over high heat. Add the hibiscus flowers, cover, reduce the heat, and simmer for 15 minutes. Remove the saucepan from the heat and strain the liquid into a bowl (the flowers can be dried to make a nutritious snack). Add the sugar to the liquid and stir with a kitchen spoon or spatula until dissolved. Let the liquid cool to room temperature.

Pour the liquid into a big glass Mason jar or into a few smaller ones, leaving about 2 inches (5 cm) of space at the top (use a funnel, if you have one, to prevent a red and sticky countertop!). Cover the jar or jars with a clean cloth,

128

kitchen towel, paper towel, or coffee filter and secure it with a rubber band or Mason jar ring. Write the brewing date on a piece of masking tape and stick it to the outside of the jar.

Let the jars sit at room temperature until the liquid starts bubbling. This may take anywhere from 3 to 10 days, depending on ambient temperature—the warmer the weather, the sooner it will start bubbling. Stir daily with a wooden spoon to prevent mold from forming. Let it bubble for a day or two and then taste it. The taste should be more tart and less sweet. If it's still on the sweeter side, let it bubble another couple of days and taste it again.

Once you like the taste, bottle it in serving-size bottles and refrigerate it. This fermented beverage is even livelier than most, so consider bottling in thick glass or BPA-free plastic bottles or heed the recommendations in the longer discussion of bottling strategies on page 55. Be careful: If you handle it casually or fail to refrigerate it consistently, you may have exploding bottles on your hands!

129

GRAPE SODA

As a child in Mexico, Raquel used to love a grape soda called Grapette. It came in a very small glass bottle and tasted like heaven! Grapette eventually disappeared, but whenever she thinks about it these days, she gets a warm longing feeling of childhood. Today's sodas are filled with artificial flavors and high fructose corn syrup and have no nutritional benefit. Making this improved version brings back happy memories!

YIELD: 4 TO 5 SERVINGS (8 OUNCES, OR 250 ML, EACH)

1 quart (1 L) Water Kefir (see page 96)

¼ to ½ cup (40 to 75 g) frozen grapes or (60 to 125 ml) grape juice

Pour the strained water kefir into lidded Mason jars, flip-top Grolsch-style bottles, or old kombucha bottles. Add the grapes or grape juice and close the lids. Write the brewing date on a piece of masking tape and stick it to the outside of the jars or bottles.

Let it sit at room temperature for 24 to 48 hours. This is the secondary fermentation. Secondary fermentation kefir can be very potent, so be careful when opening the bottles. Gas buildup can be extreme and explosions can occur! To prevent accidents, it is a good idea to refrigerate the bottles for a couple of hours before opening.

FRUITY SODA

If you find yourself with more fruit than you know what to do with, here's a good way to do something interesting with it.

YIELD: 7 SERVINGS (8 OUNCES, OR 250 ML, EACH)

4 cups (900 g) chopped seasonal fruits

7 cups (1.75 L) filtered water

½ cup (100 g) granulated sugar

Peel any fruits that you would typically peel, including oranges, grapefruits, prickly pears, mango, melon, pineapple, and watermelon. You don't need to peel any other fruits, such as apples, pears, and grapes. Chop the fruit into 4 cups (900 g) of ½-inch (1.5 cm) chunks.

Warm 2 cups (500 ml) of water in a pot over low heat. Stir in the sugar until dissolved. Transfer to a big ceramic or glass container or separate into two wide mouth Mason jars. Add the remaining 5 cups (1.25 L) of water. Stir in the chopped fruit.

Cover with a clean cloth, kitchen towel, paper towel, or coffee filter and secure it with a rubber band or Mason jar ring. Write the brewing date on a piece of masking tape and stick it to the outside of the jar.

Three times a day, open the jar, stir vigorously, and replace the cover. Within 3 to 7 days, there will be a lot of bubbling. Stir every day to prevent mold.

Once the bubbling has peaked and has just started to die down, strain out the fruit. Bottle the soda.

131

LEMONGINA/ LIMEGINA

This is an excellent sports drink containing electrolytes, vitamins, and some protein. It tastes like lemon or lime soda, but not as sweet. It is highly recommended after exercise or on a hot summer day!

YIELD: 4 SERVINGS (8 OUNCES, OR 250 ML, EACH)

1 quart (1 L) filtered water

½ cup (100 g) granulated sugar

Pinch of sea salt

Juice of 4 lemons, limes, or a combination

½ cup (125 ml) live Whey (see page 91)

¼ cup (65 g) frozen raspberries (optional)

Warm 1 pint (500 ml) of water in a pot over low heat. Stir in the sugar and salt until dissolved. Remove from the heat, add the remaining 1 pint (500 ml) of water, and let it cool down below body temperature. Add the lemon juice, whey, and raspberries (if using).

Pour the Lemongina into a glass or ceramic jar and close the lid and shake. Write the brewing date on a piece of masking tape and stick it to the outside of the jar.

Let it sit at room temperature for 3 to 7 days, depending on the temperature. Agitate at least once a day to prevent mold from forming. Begin tasting at the first sign of bubbles. It is done when it is fizzy and sour and tangy.

Refrigerate once it reaches desired taste. The raspberries may be removed or left in.

ORANGINA

For Raquel, Orangina instantly conjures memories of carefree teenage summers in France, trying to practice her French while ordering Orangina and *croque monsieurs*. Too young for wine and not having yet the acquired taste for espresso, Orangina was her beverage of choice.

A few years back, she stumbled upon the Orangina recipe in Sally Fallon's book, *Nourishing Traditions*. Postcards from cafes and streets in France immediately flooded her mind. Orangina as a probiotic healthy beverage—what could be better?

**YIELD: 4 SERVINGS
(8 OUNCES,
OR 250 ML, EACH)**

2 cups (500 ml) orange juice

Pinch of sea salt

2 tablespoons (30 ml)
Whey (see page 91)
or 1 tablespoon (15 g)
milk kefir grains

Juice of 1 lemon or lime

2 cups (500 ml)
filtered water

Combine all the ingredients in a glass or ceramic jar. Cover with the lid. Write the brewing date on a piece of masking tape and stick it to the outside of the jar.

Let it sit at room temperature for at least 2 to 3 days or until it gets fizzy.

If you added kefir grains instead of whey, strain them out, rinse them with nonchlorinated water, and refresh them with fresh milk.

Transfer the Orangina to the refrigerator. Let cool and serve.

FRUIT JUICE SODAS

David Asher, author of *The Art of Natural Cheesemaking*, suggests using milk kefir grains to ferment fruit juices. It's an easy method, and you'll be amazed at the end results. The taste is very special, and if left longer, it starts to resemble a light sparkling wine. For the healthiest results, consider using fresh-squeezed juices instead of pasteurized juices from the supermarket. Pasteurization destroys the enzymes and some of the vitamins that make fruit healthy. Fermenting brings some of them back, but the more you start with, the better.

YIELD: 1 QUART (1 L)

1 quart (1 L) fruit juice, such as apple, grape, orange, pear, or mango

1 tablespoon (15 g) milk kefir grains, rinsed with filtered water

Pour the fruit juice into a BPA-free plastic bottle or glass jar. Add the kefir grains and mix well by stirring or closing and shaking. Write the brewing date on a piece of masking tape and stick it to the outside of the jar.

Let it rest at room temperature from 1 to 3 days, depending on the temperature. Open the jar or bottle daily to release gas. Taste periodically and replace the cover if not yet done. Refrigerate when you like the taste, before the bubbling action dies down.

APPLE CIDER SODA

See the Apple Cider recipe on page 154. Apple Cider Soda is the first phase! From there you can move on to hard ciders and vinegars.

135

COCONUT SODA KEFIR

Coconut water is a great drink for when you need to hydrate because of its electrolyte content. Kefir grains add the benefits of fermentation, making this a refreshing and nutritive drink, perfect after workouts or on a hot summer day. It tastes refreshingly tropical. Follow the recipe for Water Kefir on page 96, but use coconut water (fresh or store-bought) instead of filtered water.

Remember that after making a batch of coconut water kefir or any other unusual kefir with water kefir grains, it is best to make a batch of water kefir using plain sugar water to give the kefir grains a chance to get back to normal.

If you find that the coconut soda is not sweet or bubbly enough, you can add a sweetener of your choice before fermenting or for a secondary ferment when you bottle it. Coconut sugar is one obvious choice; plain cane sugar, panela, and maple syrup would also work well.

BEERS, GRAINS, AND ROOTS

Naming fermented drinks is complicated. Sometimes, the same sort of drink arises independently in different parts of the world, leading to multiple names.

Sometimes, a drink gets multiple names in a single place. Kombucha and its many names is a great example of this phenomenon. The same thing happens with beer and wine too.

KHADI (SOUTH AFRICAN BEER)   143

BREAD KVASS   144

REJUVELAC   146

ROOT(S) BEER   148

GINGER BEER   150

BEER vs. WINE

The next two chapters are about beers and wines. The question of what is a beer and what is a wine highlights the complexity, locality, and sometimes arbitrariness of fermented drink naming (and of fermented foods in general, and, in fact, of all foods!).

Many people believe that alcoholic ferments of grains are beers, and alcohol ferments of fruits are wines. But this is a convention rather than a rule. And there are many drinks that don't fit this dichotomy, containing neither grain nor fruit as a base; there are also a few alcohol ferments that include both grain and fruit. Whether these end up being grouped with beers or having beer-like names (such as ale), being grouped with wines, or having their own categories altogether is a matter of history, accident, and sometimes of other factors such as alcohol content.

Here's a proposal for how to distinguish between beers and wines:

1. Some liquids contain most of their carbohydrates as simple sugars—monosaccharides such as glucose and fructose. Grape juice, apple juice, honey, and cactus juice are examples. Yeast can ferment simple sugars directly, so these liquids, full-strength or diluted with water, can be fermented straightforwardly and quickly with the addition of some yeast or often just by relying on ambient wild yeast and "spontaneous" fermentation.

2. Some liquids also contain disaccharides, or complex sugars, such as sucrose (table sugar), lactose (milk sugar), and maltose. Yeasts produce enzymes that digest these complex sugars into simple sugars; this clears the path for the simple sugars to be fermented into alcohol, as above. The first step, breaking down the complex sugars into simple sugars, takes some extra time, but other than that, there are no additional measures that a human needs to take to ferment these liquids. Kombucha, milk kefir, and (sometimes) water kefir fall into this category, being ferments of sucrose and lactose, although since these cultures contain bacteria in addition to yeast, most of the alcohol that develops in these is converted into acid.

Note that jun, kombucha's lesser-known cousin, starts with honey rather than sugar. That puts jun in the first category because honey contains mostly simple sugars. This explains why Jun ferments quicker than kombucha—it has one fewer step in its journey. Similarly, water kefir made with monosaccharides such as honey and fruit juice would also be in the first category. As another example, honey mead ferments more quickly than maple syrup mead (acerglyn) because honey contains mainly monosaccharides and maple syrup contains a lot more disaccharides.

3. Liquids in a third category contain substantial amounts of complex carbohydrates (starches). Typical grain ferments (beers) start off this way, as a starchy mash of grains. Yeast is not able to act on these starches directly, so some intermediate processing is necessary to break the starches down into sugars. In the case of beer, the breakdown is accomplished through heat. In some other

140

cases, the process is helped along by the addition of enzymes from other sources.

This breakdown can be accomplished in surprising ways. For example, sometimes human saliva plays a role: Saliva contains exactly the right enzymes for breaking down starch into sugar. You can confirm this by chewing on a cracker for a while; it will start to taste sweet. Some traditional beers are started in just this way, by having people chew on starchy plant material and then spit it into a vessel of some sort, where the starch continues to break down. In this book, we do not include any recipes employing human saliva, but if you are inclined to go down this road, we strongly recommend that any saliva-catalyzed breakdown be followed by a good long boil, for sanitary purposes! And you would not be betraying tradition by boiling your wort; many preparations include a boil step.

We propose that processes following pattern 1, involving mostly simple sugars, be called the wine family, and that processes following pattern 3, involving a preliminary breakdown of starches, be the beer family. Pattern 2 falls right in the middle.

Another observation is that in general, drinks following pattern 1 tend to be the least yeasty in flavor, and drinks following pattern 3 tend to be the most yeasty in flavor.

In practice, these categories may not matter much because names and categories for important drinks have already been established. But if you invent a new drink, these categories might help you decide what to call it.

BEER

Beers are generally grain ferments—most often ferments of true grains such as barley and wheat and corn and their relatives, but also sometimes ferments of pseudograins such as buckwheat, amaranth, and quinoa. Occasionally, beers can also be ferments of other starchy materials such as cassava root.

Grain beers can be divided very roughly into three categories:

- Lagers are fermented at cooler temperatures (around 50°F, or 10°C); specific yeasts adapted to these temperatures are added by the brewer.

- Ales are fermented at room temperature, give or take; the brewer adds yeasts that do well in that temperature range. Ales also generally contain more hops than lagers. Hops adds bitterness and serves as a preservative.

- Finally, wild beers are brewed at various temperatures, often around room temperature, using at least partly wild yeast—this means that the brewing happens in open containers for some period of time, and whatever yeast happen to be floating around in the air find their way into the soup, along with some bacteria, and help with the fermenting. These beers often have some sour flavors to them, thanks to the particular microbes. Regional variations in microbes can lead to regional variations in wild beers; Belgium is well known for its wild yeast grain beers, which sometimes also have fruit added to them. Yeasts and bacteria can take residence in the walls of buildings, so beers brewed in particular brewery buildings over the years often have significant consistency from batch to batch, despite being wild.

Wild beers have fallen out of favor over the last several centuries, for a few reasons. Recently, yeast has been selectively bred, allowing humans to choose the characteristics of the yeast that ferments their beer. Also, beer-making has moved from being a small-scale activity to being a major industry (more than 100 billion dollars in the United States alone in 2015). Consistency and predictability are key to industrial production of anything. Using carefully chosen yeasts makes things significantly more predictable than they would be using wild yeasts.

Some beers contain added fruit, either in the form of whole fruit or fruit juice or syrup. Often, the fruit is added as part of a secondary fermentation (see page 112). And in many common cases, as with fruit lambics, the predominant character is still that of beer. So there's little disagreement that these are beers, despite the fact that they contain fruit and fruit sugars.

In English-speaking countries, some strong ales are known as barley wines, or barleywines. (Interestingly, this naming existed in Ancient Greece as well.) Sometimes, drink naming like this is simply a matter of tradition. In other cases, it may have something to do with alcohol content and government regulations. Strong ales can have an alcohol content more typical of wine (10%) than of beer (5%) and are often taxed more heavily than normal beers; they are often consumed in wine glasses, in wine-like quantities. Calling them wines makes some sort of sense by those measures.

There are also alcoholic fermented drinks that are made from neither grains nor fruit. Nearly any liquid containing sugar can be fermented.

Some traditional American and European drinks with names such as beer and ale have been fermented regularly for centuries, sometimes for tonic or therapeutic purposes. Some of these have names that we may have heard, including ginger ale and root beer. The modern versions may not contain any ginger or roots at all and may not be fermented; bubbles can be added to drinks quickly by injecting carbon dioxide gas into them. Tartness can be added in the form of phosphoric acid, which has been implicated in osteoporosis and heart disease.

There are also traditional drinks from other cultures that are often grouped with beers, including pulque and cassava beer. The beer association may be due to their yeasty flavor and their relatively low alcohol, or it may simply be because English does not have categories for every ferment.

In this book, we do not provide recipes for typical barley-and-hops beers. This process involves many steps and can involve enough equipment that it is not ideally suited to a casual experimenter in a typical home kitchen. Instead, we provide recipes for a few traditional beers that are easier to make at home.

KHADI
(SOUTH AFRICAN BEER)

RECIPE BY HENDRIK JOHANNES JACOBUS HUGH

While Raquel was on a safari at the Kalahari Desert in South Africa, the house chef, Hendrik Johannes Jacobus Hugh, showed her this recipe. It tastes just how you imagine a pineapple beer might taste. And while you're preparing your khadi, save the pineapple peels. You can use them to make Tepache, pineapple wine! (See page 178.)

**YIELD: 16 SERVINGS
(7 OUNCES,
OR 200 ML, EACH)**

1½ cups (90 g) wheat bran

4 quarts (4 L) lukewarm filtered water, plus enough to cover the wheat bran

3 cups (600 g) granulated sugar

⅓ cup (25 g) dried ground ginger

1½ teaspoons (5 g) active dry yeast

½ of a freshly cut, peeled pineapple, chopped

Soak the wheat bran for at least 1 hour in enough lukewarm water to cover it and then drain.

Pour 4 quarts (4 L) of warm water into a large ceramic or glass pot, add the sugar, and stir until dissolved. Add the ginger, yeast, pineapple, and wheat bran and stir. Cover with a clean cloth or kitchen towel and secure it with a large rubber band. Write the brewing date on a piece of masking tape and stick it to the outside of pot.

Let it sit at room temperature for 2 to 3 days, depending on the temperature. Once it is bubbly and smells like beer, strain and serve it or refrigerate it, covered.

143

BREAD KVASS

Kvass is a fizzy drink similar to beer but generally sweeter and with a much lower alcohol content. It originated in Eastern Europe, and besides being a good probiotic, it also has nutritional properties, such as B vitamins and manganese. It is known as a hangover cure!

YIELD: 20 SERVINGS (7 OUNCES, OR 200 ML, EACH)

5 slices or 8 ounces (250 g) rye bread (see note)

5 quarts (5 L) filtered water

¼ cup (35 g) raisins

2 cups (400 g) granulated sugar

1 tablespoon (15 g) sourdough starter (see sidebar on page 145)

Toast the bread.

Bring the water to a boil in a large pot over high heat. Remove from the heat. Add the toasted bread slices and raisins. Cover the pot with a lid and let it sit overnight at room temperature or for at least 8 hours.

Strain out the bread and raisins and discard them, retaining the liquid.

Stir the sugar into the liquid until dissolved. Stir in the sourdough starter until well combined.

Cover with a clean kitchen towel and leave in a warm place—an oven with the light on works well. Let it sit for 24 hours or until foam forms on top of the brew. Once there is white foam, strain, bottle, cap, and refrigerate. After 2 days in the fridge, it is ready to drink.

CHOOSING THE BEST RYE BREAD. If buying rye bread instead of making it yourself, take a close look at ingredients list. Ingredients lists for most commercial rye breads start with enriched flour and contain less than 2% rye. Try to avoid these brands, which often also include enriched flour and preservatives, and look for more natural rye breads containing a higher percentage of rye.

144

SOURDOUGH STARTER

Sourdough starter is used to make bread using wild yeasts, thus eliminating the need to buy and use commercial yeast. Use unbleached white flour or a combination of unbleached white flour with up to half whole wheat or rye flour.

**YIELD: ABOUT
2 CUPS (500 G)**

**STARTER
INGREDIENTS**

4 ounces (125 g) flour

4 ounces (125 ml)
filtered water

**FEEDING
INGREDIENTS**

12 ounces (375 g) flour

12 ounces (375 ml)
filtered water

DAY 1

Place 4 ounces (125 g) of flour and 4 ounces (125 ml) of water in a quart (liter) jar. Mix thoroughly and close the lid.

DAY 2

Stir once or twice. Transfer to a clean jar. Close the lid.

DAY 3

Take out 2 tablespoons (30 g) of the mixture and discard it or use it to make sourdough pancakes. (There's a nice recipe in Sandor Katz's *Wild Fermentation*.) Add 2 ounces (60 g) of flour and 2 ounces (60 ml) of filtered water. Stir until blended. Transfer to a clean jar and close the lid.

DAYS 4 TO 8

Repeat the procedure for day 3 until the starter becomes quite bubbly. This means it's ready.

When you want to use the starter, put a piece of tape on the side of the jar to mark how full the jar is. Take as much of the starter from the jar as your recipe calls for. Then add flour and water back into the jar in equal amounts (by weight) to bring it back to approximately the tape mark on the jar.

If you are not going to use the starter for a while, it can be stored in the refrigerator. Feed it every week or so by removing and discarding a few tablespoons (125 g) of the starter and then stirring in flour and water as above, to maintain approximately the original volume.

REJUVELAC

Rejuvelac is a drink made from fermented, sprouted grains. Wheat berries are typical, but other whole grains such as rye and pseudo-grains such as quinoa and buckwheat are sometimes used. It tastes a bit tart, maybe like citrus, and it might have a slight yeasty or barnyard funk to it. Keep an open mind, and you may wind up loving it!

Rejuvelac is popular in raw and vegan circles. Some claim that it provides vitamins B_{12} and K_2, which are otherwise hard to find in a vegan diet; others question this claim. Regardless, rejuvelac is a good source of vitamins, enzymes, and microbes. And rejuvelac can also serve as a starter for fermented nut butters, nut cheeses, and other food projects.

Use a clean kitchen towel or sprouting top during the soaking phase. A sprouting top is a fine mesh lid, either plastic or metal. This makes the soak-rinse-drain routine quicker, and tidier than with cloth.

YIELD: 4 SERVINGS (7 OUNCES, OR 200 ML, EACH)

1 cup (250 ml) raw wheat berries or other raw, nonirradiated whole grain

Filtered water

Place the grains in a half gallon (2 L) Mason jar. Pour filtered water into the jar until the grains are submerged. Cover the jar with a clean kitchen towel, cheesecloth, or sprouting top and secure it with a rubber band or Mason jar ring. Let soak 8 to 10 hours, perhaps overnight, but not much longer. Drain through the cloth or sprouting top, rinse, and drain again.

Arrange the jar and its cover in such a way that some air circulates over the grains and so that liquid will drain as much as possible. Sally Fallon suggests laying the bottle down sideways at an angle by propping up the bottom end

146

of the jar higher than the top end, so that the liquid can drain out the top. Two to four times a day, rinse the grains, drain them, and then leave the jar on its side.

After 2 or 3 days (or sometimes sooner—it may depend on lots of factors, including the grain, room temperature, etc.), you'll notice little white tails emerging from the grains. This means that they are sprouting! Once they have sprouted, drain and rinse them.

Transfer the sprouted grains to a clean half gallon (2 L) Mason jar, add 4 cups (1 L) of water, cover with a clean cloth, kitchen towel, paper towel, or coffee filter and secure it with a rubber band or Mason jar ring.

Leave it at room temperature for 2 or 3 days until the water becomes cloudy. The cloudy water is your rejuvelac. The longer you let the liquid sit with the grains, the stronger and more sour it will get.

Start tasting your rejuvelac after the second or third day, and when you decide that it's ready, strain the sprouts out, move the liquid into a sealed bottle, and refrigerate the liquid. As you become more experienced with rejuvelac, experiment and see if you can find the level of sourness that you like most.

For best results, drink it within a week or so.

You may be able to get a second round of rejuvelac out of the same sprouted grains by adding water and letting the jar sit again. The second round may not be as strong as the first, and/or it may take longer.

ROOT(S) BEER

Root(s) beer has a very low alcohol content. What we like about this recipe is that you can incorporate any edible root you can forage or buy, or you can introduce specific roots for their therapeutic effects.

**YIELD: I2 SERVINGS
(8 OUNCES,
OR 250 ML, EACH)**

¼ cup (60 g) chopped sassafras root bark, if available; otherwise, increase the amount of the other roots

¼ cup (60 g) mixture chopped rhizomes or roots such as licorice, ginger, dandelion, or galangal

1 vanilla bean, or 2 teaspoons (10 ml) vanilla extract

½ teaspoon (1 g) wintergreen leaf or spearmint leaf

1 cinnamon stick or a dash of cinnamon powder

3 quarts (3 L) filtered water

1 cup (200 g) granulated sugar

2 tablespoons (30 ml) lime juice

½ cup (125 ml) Ginger Bug or Whey

Place the sassafras root bark, other roots, vanilla bean (if using), wintergreen leaf, and cinnamon in a large pot. Add 3 quarts (3 L) filtered water and bring to a boil over high heat. Reduce the heat to a low simmer for 15 to 20 minutes. Strain into a heatproof bowl. Stir in the sugar until dissolved. Add the vanilla extract (if using).

Let cool to body temperature or below. (Remember that too high a temperature can weaken or kill your ginger bug or whey!) Add the lime juice and ginger bug. Stir well.

Pour into flip-top Grolsch-style bottles or Mason jars with lids. (A funnel can be useful for this.) Cap or cover tightly. Write the brewing date on a piece of masking tape and stick it to the outside of each bottle or jar.

Fermentation time can range from a week to a month. As with Ginger Beer (page 150), and especially the first few times you make this recipe, it may be a good idea to include a plastic bottle as a carbonation gauge.

Start tasting after one week. Once you are satisfied with the flavor and carbonation, transfer to the refrigerator immediately. Serve chilled.

SASSAFRAS CONTROVERSY

Sassafras is a deciduous tree native to eastern North America. Its leaves, stems, bark, and roots have been used traditionally by Native Americans and by European and African settlers for centuries.

It is in fact quite a controversial plant!

A study in the 1960s showed that in large amounts, isolated components of sassafras extract can cause cancer in rats. To be fair, the same can be said of alcohol (and many other things that we consume regularly)! Regardless, because of this study, the U.S. Food and Drug Administration (FDA) restricted the use of sassafras root extracts in processed food. Also, sassafras extract, in large amounts, can be used as an ingredient when synthesizing psychedelic drugs. This undoubtedly added to the FDA's concern.

In any case, it is probably wisest not to consume sassafras daily on an ongoing basis, or in large quantities, and should it should probably be avoided by women who are pregnant or lactating. If you are in doubt, do some research for yourself, and/or ask your doctor.

Having said this, small amounts of whole sassafras have been used traditionally for centuries. Some of the reported beneficial uses of sassafras tea and sassafras root beer include, among other things: as a detox, as an analgesic, as an anti-inflammatory and anti-rheumatic, for help with painful menstruation, for help with urinary tract and prostate disorders, for help with skin ailments, and for help with eye infections and respiratory problems. Sassafras is also used to make *filé*, a seasoning used in native and Creole recipes including gumbo.

GINGER BEER

Ginger beer, or ginger ale, is a refreshing fizzy drink with a kick. It contains almost no alcohol and does not require commercial yeast to brew. Once you master making Ginger Bug, this recipe is easy and inexpensive to make. It doesn't require any specialized equipment. And it's a "beer" for the whole family to enjoy.

This recipe is another one for which you might want to use a small plastic soda bottle among the other bottles and jars. By squeezing the plastic bottle, you can assess how much carbonation has built up. When the plastic bottle has become hard, it's time to put all the bottles in the refrigerator to curtail the fermentation.

YIELD: 16 SERVINGS (8 OUNCES, OR 250 ML, EACH)

2 to 3 inches (5 to 8 cm) fresh ginger, peeled if not organic

4 quarts (4 L) filtered water

1½ cups (400 g) granulated sugar

Juice of 2 lemons, or 2 ounces (60 ml) packaged lemon juice

1 to 2 tablespoons (15 to 30 ml) bubbly Ginger Bug (see page 83)

Grate the ginger. Boil 2 quarts (2 L) filtered water in a pot over high heat. Stir the grated ginger and sugar into the boiling water until the sugar is dissolved. Turn off the heat. Cover and let sit for 15 minutes. Strain.

Add the remaining 2 quarts (2 L) filtered water. The resulting mixture should be body temperature or below; if it's still warmer than that, let it sit for a while until it has cooled. (Too much heat will kill the ginger bug!)

Once it has cooled sufficiently, stir in the lemon juice and ginger bug.

Pour into flip-top Grolsch-style bottles, Mason jars with lids, or other sturdy vessels of your choosing. (A funnel can be useful for this.) Cover tightly. Write the brewing date on a piece of masking tape and stick it to the outside of the bottles.

Let it ferment at room temperature for 10 to 15 days. Taste it from time to time. It should be bubbly and not too sweet. Refrigerate it once you like the taste or once it is sufficiently car-bonated. Serve chilled.

WINES, CIDERS, AND FRUITS (AND VINEGAR!)

CHAPTER ELEVEN

The first wines were necessarily simple and natural. Today, commercial winemakers often use additives that make their lives easier and that give us the big flavors and high alcohol levels that we've become accustomed to. Unfortunately, these additives can make us feel miserable the next day. Fortunately, you can prepare your own simple wines at home. Like with many home food preparation projects, you gain some control over the ingredients and health effects, and you also save money.

APPLE CIDER 1, 2, 3   154

PERRY   158

BERRY WINE   159

COUNTRY WINE   161

PRISON WINE/HOOCH   162

MEAD   164

RICE WINE   166

SPARKLING COUNTRY WINE   168

APPLE CIDER 1, 2, 3

If you have apple trees or know somebody who does, you will love these recipes. Even if you must buy apple juice, you will still love them. From one ingredient—apple juice—you can get three different drinks: Apple Cider Soda for everyone, Hard Apple Cider for alcohol drinkers, and Apple Cider Vinegar for the rest of the year.

If you want to use store-bought apple juice, make sure it doesn't contain preservatives; the main purpose of preservatives is to inhibit microbes, and microbes are key to fermentation! Clear and cloudy apple juice both work, but give slightly different results, so try whichever one appeals to you, or try both.

Note that this same method works with other juices as well. Pear cider is called perry; grape cider could be called . . . wine!

YIELD: VARIABLE

Apples, preferably organic

OR

Freshly-pressed apple juice, preferably organic and preservative-free

OR

Preservative-free, store-bought apple juice from the store, plus a few organic apples to juice yourself

APPLE CIDER SODA

If starting with apples, juice or blend them; strain using mesh or cheesecloth. Discard or compost the pulp.

Pour the apple juice into a ceramic or glass vessel or vessels. Fill each no more than two-thirds full. Aerate by either stirring with a spoon or closing with an airtight lid and shaking. Remove the lid and cover the vessel with a clean cloth, kitchen towel, paper towel, or coffee filter, secured with a rubber band. Write the date on a piece of masking tape and stick it to the outside of the jar.

154

Let it sit at room temperature.

At some point within several days, there will be a lot of bubbling. Ambient temperature has a big effect on how soon this happens. Until the bubbling has started, stir vigorously or shake three times a day and then cover as before. Aerating the juice like this helps wild yeast find it, and it prevents mold from taking hold on the surface.

Once the bubbling has peaked and started to slow down, bottle the soda in BPA-free plastic containers or in suitable glass containers, cover or cap tightly, and refrigerate. Plastic bottles may be safer because they handle pressure in a more predictable and measurable way. (See page 55 for a longer discussion of bottling strategies.)

When bottling, you may retain the sediment or discard it as desired. If you want to keep as much as possible of the sediment, stir the cider gently before bottling to distribute it evenly. Don't stir too hard, though, or you will lose a lot of the bubbles. To remove the sediment, filter the liquid through a fine mesh strainer or cheesecloth during bottling; alternatively, allow the sediment to settle to the bottom and then pour off the liquid, or siphon it off the top when ready to drink, or use any other method that seems convenient. (Siphoning has the advantage of disrupting the cider the least, thus retaining the most bubbles.) Do be aware that the sediment contains yeast, which contains B vitamins and some protein, so for maximum health benefit, retain the sediment in the drink or perhaps find some other way to consume it, such as in salad dressing.

Do not shake Apple Cider Soda prior to opening the container. If you do, you will lose a lot of your soda when you open the bottle!

HARD APPLE CIDER

Follow the steps for making Apple Cider Soda until it starts bubbling. If you have a container with an airlock, transfer the soda to this container as soon as it starts bubbling. If you don't have a container with an airlock, wait until the bubbling has mostly died down and then put the cider it in a sealed container and relieve pressure manually every few days by opening the cap a bit and then closing it tight.

Let the bottle sit at room temperature, closed, for up to 1 month.

Remove the sediment as instructed above, if desired. Bottle and refrigerate.

APPLE CIDER VINEGAR

You can make apple cider vinegar (or any kind of fruit vinegar, including grape vinegar) by leaving Apple Cider Soda, Hard Apple Cider, or any fruit wine exposed to air at room temperature for a long time.

Follow all the steps for making Apple Cider Soda and just let it keep fermenting, covered with a clean cloth, kitchen towel, paper towel, or coffee filter and sealed with a rubber band, at room temperature (rather than bottling after the bubbling slows down). Continue stirring every day (to prevent mold from forming on top) and tasting it occasionally. Once it has soured and the bubbling has ceased (after a week or much longer), you may optionally add as much

as ¼ cup (60 ml) of existing raw apple cider vinegar per quart (liter) to speed up the rest of the process. Be sure to leave your liquid far from any other open fermenting culture to prevent cross-contamination. You can let it ferment for up to a year at room temperature. Taste it from time to time. It is done when there is no longer any trace of sweetness.

Once it's done, apple cider vinegar is best bottled in capped glass containers; glass is ideal for long-term storage of acidic liquids, and carbon dioxide pressure buildup is not a concern with vinegar, since all the sugar is gone and there's very little chemical reaction still happening.

Note that vinegar you make this way will not necessarily be as strong as vinegar that you buy at the store, which is adjusted to a standardized strength. This means that in recipes that rely on specific acidity levels for reasons of chemistry or food safety (such as canning), store-bought vinegar is best.

JOHNNY APPLESEED'S APPLES

Johnny Appleseed (born John Chapman, 1774, in Leominster, MA) was an American frontier folk hero, famous for planting great numbers of apple trees and preaching the gospel. An interesting thing about apples is that they do not breed true; for reasons that can be explained by theories of genetics, the seeds from the most wonderful-tasting apple are likely to develop into trees with very different, less delightful, and, in fact, quite sour apples. The way to get predictable apples is to clone trees, and the best way to do that is to graft branches from one tree onto another.

But this is not what Johnny Appleseed was doing. He was planting seeds, which would likely result in sour apples. And the most likely use for common sour apples would be . . . for making cider!

PERRY

Once you have mastered Apple Cider, Perry will be easy because it's made the same way. In fact, the same method can be applied to quince juice and many other juices. Pear soda and perry start off tasting decidedly pear-like; the longer perry ferments, the subtler the pear flavor will become.

Follow the recipe for Apple Cider on page 154. Substitute pears for the apples, and if you want to, add some spices, such as cinnamon, allspice, nutmeg, or cloves, in moderation.

Note that some of the timing might be a little different. Move from step to step based on what you see and taste, rather than basing it on any strict timetable.

BERRY WINE

As we've seen by now, there are many ways to make fruit wine. This method gives the wild yeast a day or two and then adds in some packaged yeast. It should result in a nice, clean berry wine, with little "funk."

YIELD: 8 TO 10 SERVINGS

4 pounds (2 kg) frozen ripe berries

4 quarts (4 L) filtered water

2 pounds (1 kg) granulated sugar

1 package (0.2 ounces, or 5 g) wine yeast

Thaw the berries and mash them up in a crock or other large vessel.

Boil 2 quarts (2 L) of water in a stockpot. Add the sugar and stir until dissolved. Add the remaining 2 quarts (2 L) of water and continue to stir. Once it reaches warm room temperature, add the water to the berries in a large (at least 2 gallons [8 L]) crock or glass jar. Cover with a clean cloth or kitchen towel and secure it with a rubber band. Write the date on a piece of masking tape and stick it to the outside of the vessel.

Let it sit at room temperature.

After 24 to 48 hours, add the yeast and stir twice daily for 1 week, keeping it covered with clean cloth when not stirring.

Strain the liquid and pour into one or more clean carboys or jugs. Cap with airlocks. Write the date on a piece of masking tape and stick it to the outside of the jug(s). Let it sit at room temperature for at least 1 month.

After a month or more, there will be sediment and yeast at the bottom of the jugs. Decant or siphon the wine into new clean bottles. Wine bottles or other flip-top bottles work well. Cap the bottles and let them sit at room temperature for at least 3 months.

159

COUNTRY WINE

Country wine is a general term for wine made from fruit, generally any kind of fruit except for grapes. If you find yourself with an overabundance of fruit and want to make a fun drink for yourself, your family, and your guests, this might be just the thing.

YIELD: 6 TO 8 SERVINGS (8 OUNCES, OR 250 ML, EACH)

2 quarts (2 L) filtered water

2 cups (400 g) granulated sugar

2 cups (450 g) finely chopped, unpeeled seasonal fruit

Boil the water in large pot over high heat. Stir in the sugar until dissolved. Turn off the heat. Let cool to body temperature or below. Transfer to a large crock or glass jar. Add the fruit.

Cover with a clean cloth, kitchen towel, paper towel, or coffee filter and secure it with a rubber band. Write the date on a piece of masking tape and stick it to the outside of the vessel.

Let it sit at room temperature. Uncover and stir vigorously 3 times a day every day. Cover.

Bubbling action should start within 24 to 72 hours. Each time you stir, more bubbles should appear. On day 5 or later (depending on the temperature), when the bubbling action slows, strain out the fruit and transfer the liquid into a clean glass jug. Close with an airlock. Leave for several weeks until the bubbling has died down completely. Decant or siphon off the liquid, leaving behind as much of the sediment as possible. (Experiment with eating the sediment if you wish.) You can drink the wine immediately; otherwise, bottle it in wine bottles, flip-top Grolsch-style bottles, clean kombucha bottles, or Mason jars and refrigerate.

PRISON WINE/ HOOCH

Prison wine is the embodiment of the proverb, "Necessity is the mother of invention." If you are bored, desperate, and/or clever enough, you can figure out how to make wine from available materials. If you can get your hands on fruit juice, fruit, packets of sugar, water, bowls, and bags, you can make wine.

YIELD: 3 SERVINGS (8 OUNCES, OR 250 ML, EACH)

1 cup (225 g) chopped, ripe fruit

3 cups (750 ml) fruit juice

¼ cup (50 g) granulated sugar

The first step is to pre-ferment the fruit: Place it in a bowl, cover the bowl with a clean cloth or kitchen towel, and secure it with a rubber band to dissuade fruit flies. Leave the bowl of fruit at room temperature for 24 to 48 hours. The fruit should begin to smell very ripe, giving off an almost alcoholic aroma.

Once fruit is pre-fermented, pour the fruit juice in a large mixing bowl. Add the sugar and stir to dissolve. Add the fruit.

Write the date on the outside of a clean zip-top bag. Pour the contents of the jar (fruit and juice) into the bag and close it.

Let it sit at room temperature. Open every day for the first 5 days and release the gas. Close and give it a gentle squeeze to mix it up. Continue to ferment for 1 to 2 weeks, tasting every few days. After a couple of weeks, you will begin to taste the alcohol. If the bag inflates too much, open it again and let the gas out. Once it reaches desired taste, strain and drink the wine. Bottle and refrigerate any leftover wine.

MEAD

Mead is certainly among the oldest alcoholic beverages, dating back to around 9000 BCE by some estimates. It is also one of the easiest to brew. This recipe is for a wild mead, meaning that there is no added yeast.

One part honey to four parts water, by weight, is a good starting point. Once you've made it a few times, try varying the ratio if you like. A bit more honey will result in a stronger and/or sweeter mead.

If you add spices, herbs, and roots, then your mead becomes a variation known as metheglin, which has the same root as *medicine*. Meads enhanced with medicinal plants have been used as medicines for a long time.

YIELD: I GALLON (4 L)

2 pounds (1 kg) raw honey

4 quarts (4 L) filtered water

Finely chopped herbs, spices, fruit peels, dried edible flowers, or other flavorings of your choice, such as bay leaves, rosemary, ginger, citrus peels, turmeric, etc. (optional)

Dissolve the honey in the water. Pour into a large ceramic or wide mouth glass vessel. Add the herbs (if using) and stir. Cover the vessel with a clean cloth or kitchen towel and secure it with a rubber band. Write the date on a piece of masking tape on the outside of the jar.

Let it sit at room temperature. Stir vigorously 3 times a day.

There will be bubbling action during the first week. Once the bubbling action begins to die down, strain and transfer to a jug or jugs and close with an airlock. Leave for 2 to 4 weeks, depending on temperature, or much longer. For a young mead, drink it when there are no more bubbles. The longer you wait after that, the more alcohol it will contain and the less sweet it will be. If you ferment it long enough, the honey

flavor will recede into the background, and it will start to taste almost like dry white wine.

To store, syphon the liquid and pour it into clean bottles or jars. Store the bottles or jars in a cool place for weeks or months.

RICE WINE

Variations on sticky rice and rice wine have been popular in East Asia for a long time. This recipe emphasizes the wine, but the rice is part of the fun, too. The leftover sweet rice can be eaten for dessert, but it is also popular for breakfast, perhaps with a boiled egg. This seems like a nice way to ease into the day!

YIELD: VARIES

6 cups (1.5 L) filtered water, divided

2 cups (500 g) uncooked sticky rice or glutinous rice

1 Shanghai yeast ball or rice wine yeast ball

Warm 3 cups (750 ml) of water in a pot over low heat to body temperature. Remove from the heat, add the rice to the pot, cover, and soak for one hour or more. Rinse and drain.

Boil the remaining 3 cups (750 ml) water in a pot. Add the rice, lower heat to a simmer, cover, and cook 15 to 20 minutes until all the water is absorbed.

Spread out the cooked sticky rice in a large bowl to cool to room temperature.

Pulverize the yeast ball with your hands and spread over the rice.

Cover the bowl with plastic wrap and take whatever measures you can to keep the bowl at around 73°F (23°C). If it is warmer or colder, it will still ferment, but this is the best temperature. To control the temperature, wrap the bowl in a large towel and put it in a big cooler or some other enclosed space (like your oven, if you aren't using it!). After 4 to 5 days, it should be full of liquid. If not, let it sit for a few more days.

That liquid is the rice wine. Once there is a good amount of it, pour it into a Mason jar. Spoon the rice into a cheesecloth and squeeze

166

it through a strainer to get more of the liquid, which can be added into the same jar.

Close the jar with a lid and refrigerate it. Serve chilled.

Save the sticky rice in the refrigerator and eat it as a dessert or as a zingy breakfast porridge.

SPARKLING COUNTRY WINE

Using a secondary fermentation, we transform country wine into country champagne!

YIELD: A LITTLE MORE THAN 2 QUARTS (2 L)

SYRUP

1 cup (250 ml) filtered water

½ cup (100 g) granulated sugar

WINE

1 cup (250 ml) syrup

2 quarts (2 L) Country Wine (page 161), Berry Wine (page 159), or Hooch (page 162)

SYRUP

Heat the water over low heat in a small saucepan. Stir in the sugar until dissolved. Remove from the heat and let cool to body temperature or below.

WINE

Mix the syrup and the wine. Pour the sweetened wine into flip-top Grolsch-style or beer bottles and cap. Store at room temperature (65°F to 70°F [18°C to 21°C]) for 5 to 10 days. After 5 days, open one bottle, observe the level of carbonation, and taste it. If it is not bubbly, close the bottle, leave it for another few days, and try again then. Repeat until it's sparkling and bubby, at which point it is ready to drink or refrigerate. When opening, be careful not to shake vigorously, as it can make a mess!

MEXICAN
PRE-HISPANIC
DRINKS

As did many cultures, pre-Hispanic peoples preserved their food via fermentation, often via fermented drinks. That's how they saved corn, fruit, and other agricultural products, giving them rich flavors and increased nutritional value along the way.

PULQUE   175

COLONCHE   176

TEPACHE   178

TEJUINO   181

As with many ancestral traditions, the processes for preparing fermented drinks are simple, inexpensive, and safe, inhibiting the growth of pathogenic bacteria.

It is sad to see these beverages become scarcer in Mexico and the rest of the world as people turn to mass-produced sugary sodas. You can make these for yourself at home instead of buying factory-produced sodas.

Some of the most popular Mexican pre-Hispanic fermented drinks are pulque (made from aguamiel, the sap of the maguey), tepache (made from pineapple and piloncillo sugar), tejuino (from nixtamal or corn masa), and colonche (made from prickly pear).

HISTORY OF PULQUE

Before beer, there was pulque.

In pre-Hispanic times, pulque was the drink of the Gods. It was consumed by priests and members of the royal family during their rituals. Old men and women, retired from active life, were also allowed to drink and enjoy it. And prisoners could inebriate themselves with it before being put to death.

Drinking pulque was generally forbidden for anybody else, and being drunk was a punishable offense. Repeat offenders were condemned to die—beaten, stoned, or hanged. Only on special occasions, such as the festivities for the Gods of Wine, were all the citizens, including children, allowed to drink pulque until drunk.

After the Spanish conquest, punishments for drinking pulque ended, so indigenous people continued to drink it, not only to get drunk, but as a dietary supplement. Sometimes, pulque was the only drink available, and being a fermented drink, it contained healthful vitamins and enzymes. Because it was unfiltered, it contained some amounts of protein too, from the yeast.

During this time, pulque commerce increased until it became a profitable local business. But after the Mexican Revolution, pulque faced its nemesis: beer, which was easier and cheaper to manufacture, hence more profitable. Barley and wheat displaced maguey. To support the beer brewing industry, the Mexican government imposed new regulations discouraging pulque commerce and even propagated a rumor that pulque was made using feces as a starter.

A tough competitor, negative propaganda, and the difficulty of transport and distribution almost led to the demise of pulque. The number of *pulquerías* (pulque bars) in Mexico decreased from over a thousand at the beginning of the twentieth century to maybe only a hundred at the beginning of this century.

WHERE TO GET FRESH PULQUE

Distributing pulque at scale is quite difficult, as it continues to ferment even after bottling. There have been several commercial attempts, but they have failed—pulque cans have exploded in supermarket aisles! Up until now, the easiest way to enjoy pulque has been to take it fresh out of the fermentation bucket in a pulquería.

Pulquerías are now making a comeback in Mexico. And given the appetite of North Amer-

PULQUE
TERMINOLOGY

- Tlachiquero: This is someone who takes care of the maguey plant.
- Aguamiel: This is the sap of the maguey plant.
- Acocote: This is the instrument used to collect aguamiel.

icans for new foods and drinks, and the speed with which trends spread nowadays, it is only a matter of time before pulque makes its way into the bar culture north of the border. The biggest barriers are the difficulty of transporting pulque, as mentioned above, and the length of time it takes for the maguey plant to mature.

HOW PULQUE IS MADE

The process of making pulque begins with the maguey plant, which takes 12 to 15 years to fully develop.

Just when the cactus is about to flower, the tlachiquero cuts the flower stem. (Don't feel bad for the maguey—it can only live for a limited time after it starts to flower, whether or not its flower stem is cut.) Several months after the flower stem is cut, the tlachiquero will scrape the base of the maguey, and as the plant tries to heal itself, it will produce aguamiel. The tlachiquero uses the acocote to extract the aguamiel and pour it into a tub.

After extraction, the tlachiquero will again scrape the surface with a knife for a new batch of aguamiel. If the plant is left with no wound, then there will be no aguamiel, as the maguey heals itself by producing the sap. Each maguey plant can produce several batches of aguamiel per day, every day for up to a year, before the plant dies.

The freshly collected sap goes straight into a big bucket of previously-fermented aguamiel called the seed or pulque mother. Fermentation starts immediately. As aguamiel is being poured into the bucket, it is aerated. Duration for fermentation depends on the producer. It can be hours or days.

MAKING YOUR OWN PULQUE

Yes, you can turn your kitchen into a pulquería. The alcohol content may not be as high as traditionally produced pulque, but at least you can sample the taste.

For the best practical approximation, we recommend buying unheated, unfiltered, concentrated maguey sap and mixing it with water, as described below. The best source we've found is the Villa de Patos brand.

NOTE ON AGAVE NECTAR: Commercial agave nectar is typically heated, filtered, and generally quite processed. It will ferment just like any sweet liquid will, but the results will not be pulque.

PULQUE

3 cups (750 ml) filtered water

1 cup (325 g) unrefined maguey sweet sap (not agave nectar)

Pour the water into a Mason jar. Add the maguey sap and stir until dissolved. Cover the jar with a clean cloth, kitchen towel, paper towel, or coffee filter and secure it with a rubber band or Mason jar ring. Write the brewing date on a piece of masking tape and stick it to the outside of the jar.

Let it sit at room temperature for 5 days up to 3 weeks, depending on ambient temperature.

You can start tasting at day 3. It should start tasting sour. Once you like the flavor, transfer to bottles. Plastic BPA-free bottles are highly recommended. Remember that pulque continues to ferment! Close tightly and refrigerate.

VARIATION: PULQUE WITH MILK KEFIR GRAINS

Adding milk kefir grains can help your fermentation along. David Asher, author of *The Art of Natural Cheesemaking*, did this with raw aguamiel de maguey during a visit to Mexico, and he passed on his recipe:

Add 1 teaspoon of milk kefir grains previously rinsed in nonchlorinated water to 1 cup (325 g) of aguamiel de maguey and 3 cups (750 ml) of water, as above. Close the lid and let it ferment for 24 to 72 hours, depending on the temperature. Once the aguamiel is fermented, it will be thicker and taste of pulque.

175

COLONCHE

Colonche is a pre-Hispanic drink made by fermenting the pulp of the red prickly pear fruit. Thus, colonche is another cactus wine. This version is by Ernesto Fato.

YIELD: 8 SERVINGS

4½ pounds (2 kg) mature red prickly pears

¼ cup (60 ml) lukewarm water

2 grams dry yeast

¼ cup (50 g) sugar

Peel each prickly pear by cutting off the ends, sticking a fork in it, slitting the skin from end to end, and removing it. Crush the fruit with a mortar and pestle, trying to avoid breaking the seeds. Breaking the seeds sours the juice. (Using a blender is not recommended for this reason.)

Strain the juice into a mixing bowl using a cloth or strainer.

In another bowl, stir together the warm (around body temperature) water and yeast. Stir in the sugar until dissolved. Pour the yeast mixture into a glass or ceramic container. Stir the prickly pear juice into the yeast mixture. Cover with a clean cloth, kitchen towel, paper towel, or coffee filter and secure it with a rubber band. Write the brewing date on a piece of masking tape and stick it to the outside of the container.

Let it sit at room temperature for 3 to 5 days, depending on the temperature.

Taste it. There should be an alcoholic fruity flavor. Bottle, cap, and refrigerate it when it's ready. Serve chilled.

TEPACHE

Tepache, a fermented pineapple beverage, is a signature drink for Mexicans. In some parts of Mexico, if you are lucky, you may still find tepache vendors in the streets, but its popularity has been declining among younger generations. So you can imagine Raquel's joyful surprise when she stumbled upon a 2014 *Bon Appetit* article titled "Why You Should be Drinking Tepache Cocktails!" As a nod to her pre-Hispanic roots, she is happy to share her Tepache recipe here, for your next cocktail.

YIELD: ABOUT 4 TO 6 SERVINGS, DEPENDING ON THE SIZE OF THE PINEAPPLE

Outer peel of 1 pineapple (eat the rest of the pineapple or refrigerate it for another use)

Filtered water

1 cup (200 g) panela or brown sugar

1 cinnamon stick

3 or 4 whole cloves and/or star anise

Place the pineapple peels in a half gallon to 1 gallon (2 to 4 L) Mason jar or ceramic container. Add filtered water to the vessel to cover the peels.

Dissolve the panela in about 1 cup (250 ml) lukewarm water and pour it into the container. Add the cinnamon and cloves. Stir. Cover with a clean cloth, kitchen towel, paper towel, or coffee filter and secure it with a rubber band. Write the brewing date on a piece of masking tape and stick it to the outside of the container.

Let it sit at room temperature for 3 to 5 days.

Try tasting on day 3. The warmer the room, the quicker it will ferment. When it starts tasting less sweet and more tart, it is done. Pour the tepache through a strainer into a jar or bottles with airtight lids. Refrigerate and serve cold.

PINEAPPLE TIPS & TRICKS

- If tepache ferments for too long and starts tasting vinegary, let it continue to ferment for a while more, and you will have a delicious pineapple vinegar!

- If you eat pineapple with any frequency, a pineapple slicer/decorer will make your life easier.

- If you are careful with the pineapple corer, you may be able to stop turning before you cut through the bottom, creating a hollow pineapple suitable for use as a mug for juice or drinks! Of course, if you want to fill it with tepache, you will need to make the tepache ahead of time using a different pineapple.

HOW TO MAKE MASA DOUGH

To make masa dough from dry masa flour, combine 3 cups (350 g) dry masa harina with 2 cups (500 ml) of water. Mix thoroughly and let sit for at least 15 minutes.

Masa dough and dry masa flour are available in many varieties. For this recipe, if you have a choice between masa for tortillas and masa for tamales, we recommend the masa for tortillas. Yellow and white masa work equally well.

We highly recommend non-GMO masa. Unfortunately, in the United States, the biggest brands are all GMO. Mexico currently bans growing GMO corn. The brand that we recommend in the United States is Bob's Red Mill. They pledge that their products are non-GMO, to the best of their knowledge. Organic products are not allowed to be GMO, so any organic masa you can find will automatically be non-GMO too.

Markets and regulations change from time to time, so if GMO is a concern for you, as it is for us, you may need to do some research.

TEJUINO

Tejuino is a pre-Hispanic fermented corn drink still popular in the western states of Mexico. It is said that *Tejuino* comes from the Nahuatl word *tecuin*, which means "to beat." Drinking tejuino creates joy, thus provoking the heart to beat faster.

**YIELD: ABOUT
3 QUARTS (3 L)**

FOR TEJUINO

3 quarts (3 L) plus
1 cup (250 ml) water

2 pounds (1 kg) piloncillo
(also called panela)

2 pounds (1 kg) wet corn masa
dough (masa preparada)

OR

3 cups (350 g) masa harina
(dry masa flour) plus
2 cups (500 ml) water

Juice of 2 limes

FOR SERVING

Ice

Sea salt

Lime juice

Bring 3 quarts (3 L) of water to a boil in pot over high heat. Stir in the piloncillo until dissolved.

Mix the masa harina with 1 cup (250 ml) of water using your hands or a food processor and add it to the piloncillo water. Stir well. Let it cool to room temperature. Add the lime juice. Pour into a glass or ceramic vessel. Cover with a clean cloth, kitchen towel, paper towel, or coffee filter and secure it with a rubber band. Write the brewing date on a piece of masking tape and stick it to the outside of the vessel.

Let it sit for 3 days at room temperature.

Pour off the liquid and save it; that is your tejuino!

Chill and serve over ice, with a bit of salt and lime juice mixed in.

FERMENTED COCKTAILS

As we've seen, fermentation and humans have a long history together, and fermented drinks have been around for a long time. Essentially all the alcohol that humans consume is the result of fermentation, either directly or concentrated via a process known as distilling.

UR-PIÑA COLADA 186

TEPACHE HIGHBALL 187

CALIENTE 188

TEPACHE SMASH 189

KOMBUCHA SANGRIA 189

KOMBUCHA MEZCAL 190

KOMBUCHA CARAJILLO 191

KOMBUCHA SHANDY 191

LOUIS CK/KANSAS CITY 192

KIMCHI BLOODY MARY 193

SAUERKRAUT MICHELADA 194

195 KIMCHI MICHELADA

196 HIBISCUS MEZCAL

196 ORANGINA MARGARITA

197 APPLE CIDER MARGARITA

197 APPLE CIDER BELLINI

199 GINGER ALE A LA MEXICANA

199 GINGER ALE CRANBERRY VODKA

Yeast is responsible for converting sugar into alcohol, but yeast itself has only a limited tolerance for alcohol; if the circumstances are right, yeast will produce enough alcohol to poison itself! Different yeasts have different thresholds. The most extreme yeasts can survive up to 25% ABV, but this is unusual. Most yeasts cannot get even close to 25%, and most fermented drinks are nowhere near this strong.

Wild fermented drinks tend to have lower alcohol contents than drinks made with domesticated yeasts, both because wild yeasts have lower tolerances and because wild ferments generally incorporate some population of acetic acid-producing bacteria. That means that while the yeast is producing alcohol, the bacteria are converting some of it into acid. Industrial wine and beer production is done under more carefully controlled conditions, and it uses domesticated cultivated yeasts developed for higher alcohol tolerances, so modern wines with alcohol concentrations of 13% or even 15% are not unusual. Beers with comparable levels of alcohol are becoming more popular too.

Wild fermented drinks are often unfiltered, while modern industrial drinks are almost always filtered. The things lost through filtering include nutrients, B vitamins among them, that may support liver function; thus unfiltered, wild drinks are likely to be easier on our bodies than industrially produced ones, both because of their lower alcohol and because they include their own "hangover helper." Remember this the next time you have a hangover!

Having said this, if we are willing to take the risk and possibly suffer the consequences, how can we get drinks with higher alcohol concentrations than are achievable via fermentation alone, even fermentation with domesticated super-yeasts?

Generally, we get stronger drinks by taking advantage of the fact that alcohol boils, or freezes, at lower temperatures than water does. This allows us to separate out alcohol and water via fractional freezing or fractional distillation.

Fractional freezing, because it requires no specials tools, is easy to do at home. Partially freeze your drink; the ice crystals that form will contain a proportionally higher concentration of water, and the remaining liquid will have a proportionally higher concentration of alcohol and other drink components. This process is known colloquially as "jacking;" if you do it with hard cider, the resulting drink is known as "applejack." You can use this technique to get higher alcohol levels, but opinions differ about how safe it is. Along with the desired ethanol, other components of the drink get concentrated too, some of them potentially problematic—methanol for instance, also known as wood alcohol, which can cause blindness and death if consumed in large amounts. If you do choose to experiment, remember that water expands when it freezes, so loosen or remove any lids or caps before trying this. Cleaning broken glass out of a freezer is not fun—we've done it!

On a larger scale, higher alcohol concentrations are generally achieved via fractional distillation. This involves heating the liquid mixture so that parts of it (fractions) evaporate, or boil off—that is, change from a liquid into a gas. Different parts boil off at different temperatures. The part that boils off in a specific temperature range is collected and cooled and condenses back into a liquid. Ethanol boils at its own distinct temperature, so by controlling the temperature and collecting the condensate, it's possible to boil off (mostly) the alcohol that we want and then condense it back into a liquid elsewhere.

What does this have to do with cocktails?

These days, cocktails are almost always made from distilled alcohol. The exception, popular with establishments that aren't licensed to sell strong alcohol, are cocktails made from wines, beers, sojus, and sakes.

Fermented drinks offer a broad range of sour and spicy flavors that beg to be turned into cocktails for the adventurous. Why not make cocktails that include fermented foods and drinks outside the usual ones?

UR-PIÑA COLADA

The modern Piña Colada, containing pineapple juice, coconut cream, and rum, is quite delicious, but can also be quite sweet, and drinking too many can lead to regrets the next day. What if we could make a probiotic version of the drink with less alcohol, less sugar, and more vitamins? We can. And we can also speculate that perhaps in the lands of coconuts and pineapple, people were drinking coconut water (fresh or fermented) alongside pineapple (fresh or fermented) without rum for quite some time, before the "official" invention of the modern Piña Colada in the nineteenth or twentieth century. We can enjoy the kinder, gentler Piña Colada today, and in fact, we can enjoy it all day, without too much risk of getting too drunk. Or we can have the best of both worlds, old and new, by combining the fermented tropical drinks with a shot of rum.

YIELD: ABOUT 12 OUNCES (375 ML)

Ice

4 ounces (125 ml) Coconut Soda Kefir (see page 136), fresh coconut water, coconut milk, or coconut cream

4 ounces (125 ml) Tepache (see page 178)

1 shot (1½ fluid ounces, or 45 ml) rum or spiced rum (optional)

Fill a cocktail shaker with ice, coconut water, tepache, and rum (if using). Shake and strain into a chilled glass with some more ice. Serve immediately.

186

TEPACHE HIGHBALL

A highball is typically a shot of a strong drink mixed into a tall glass of a softer drink. The first official highball may have been the scotch and soda, around the beginning of the twentieth century. The term *ball* was used to signify a drink of whiskey and *high* because it was served in a tall glass! The formula has spread widely since, in many variations. For something new, try this Tepache Highball.

**YIELD: ABOUT
12 OUNCES (375 ML)**

8 ounces (250 ml)
Tepache (see page 178)

1 shot (1½ fluid ounces,
or 45 ml) of mezcal

1 teaspoon aguamiel de
maguey, maple syrup, or
molasses, or to taste

Ice

1 splash of club soda

Pineapple wedge

Chapulín, ant, or worm salt,
or plain salt

Stir the tepache, mezcal, and aguamiel de maguey in a highball glass until well mixed. Fill a glass with ice and top with club soda. Add a pineapple wedge and sprinkle with salt. Serve.

(UN)COMMON MEXICAN SALTS

Enjoy these salts that have been around since pre-Hispanic times. For more information, visit www.companiadesales.com.

- *Sal de Hormiga*, also known as ant salt, is made with powdered black ants.
- *Sal de Gusano*, also known as worm salt, is made with ground up agave worms.
- *Sal de Chapulin*, also known as grasshopper salt, is made with powdered grasshoppers.

CALIENTE

Caliente is the Spanish word for "hot," and it means hot in both senses: weather and desires. This cocktail, involving tepache, ginger beer, and hot pepper sauce, can help both keep out the cold and raise your passions.

**YIELD: ABOUT
12 OUNCES (375 ML)**

Salt for rim, plain,
seasoned, or smoked

2 ounces (60 ml)
Tepache (see page 178)

8 ounces (250 ml)
Ginger Beer (see page 150)

Crushed ice

Dash of hot pepper sauce

Salt the rim of a tall glass.

Pour the tepache and ginger beer into the glass. Add crushed ice and pepper sauce. Stir and serve.

TEPACHE SMASH

We named this cocktail Tepache Smash because drinking it feels like diving into the Caribbean Sea in a hot summer day.

YIELD: ABOUT 12 OUNCES (375 ML)

8 ounces (250 ml) Tepache (see page 178)

1 shot (1½ fluid ounces, or 45 ml) of gin

Crushed ice

Pour the tepache and gin into a chilled glass. Add crushed ice. Stir and serve.

KOMBUCHA SANGRIA

Sangria is typically prepared by mixing red wine with lemonade and adding chunks of fruit. It is good for summer time when red wine alone can feel too heavy. This is a sangria twist—less sugar and more probiotic content.

YIELD: 1 SERVING

8 ounces (250 ml) unflavored Kombucha (see page 105)

2 to 4 ounces (60 to 125 ml) red wine

2 tablespoons (30 g) chopped fruit or fruit cocktail

Ice (optional)

Pour the kombucha and red wine into a large wine glass. Stir gently. Add the fruit and ice (if using). Serve.

189

KOMBUCHA MEZCAL

Mezcal is a distilled alcohol drink from the agave plant. It typically comes from one of Mexico's most beautiful states, Oaxaca. It has a smoky taste and is more complex than tequila. If mezcal is drunk by itself, it is often accompanied by some lime, orange slices, and chili powder—or even tastier with warm salt. It is best sipped and enjoyed, not chugged wildly as if at a bachelor party.

Kombucha Mezcal is perfect to introduce mezcal to your taste buds. It gives kombucha an extra kick and a hint of seduction.

Pour the kombucha and mezcal into a large wine glass. Stir gently. Add crushed ice and serve.

YIELD: I SERVING

8 ounces (250 ml)
berry-flavored Kombucha
(see page 112)

1 ounce (30 ml) mezcal

Crushed ice

KOMBUCHA CARAJILLO

We love carajillo as a digestive drink in Mexico after a big meal. A typical carajillo is prepared by mixing Licor 43 (very sweet and high alcohol content), espresso, and lots of ice.

YIELD: I SERVING

½ cup (125 ml) Coffee Kombucha or regular Kombucha (see page 113 or 105)

2 ounces (60 ml) Licor 43

Crushed ice

Pour the kombucha into an old fashioned glass. Stir in the Licor 43 and crushed ice. Serve.

KOMBUCHA SHANDY

This is a simple recipe: Add some flavored kombucha to your favorite beer. We suggest a ginger- or citrus-flavored kombucha, combined with a light beer or lager. This way, both the kombucha and the beer come through. But, of course, you are free to experiment and see what you like best.

This is a great drink for a warm summer afternoon, or for early evening, since it's not too strong. It tastes like sweet and sour beer!

YIELD: I2 OUNCES (375 ML)

6 ounces (175 ml) beer

6 ounces (175 ml) Kombucha (see page 105)

Ice (optional)

Pour the beer into a tall glass. Stir in the kombucha. Stir gently. Add ice if desired. Serve.

191

LOUIS CK/KANSAS CITY

Combining the aperitif and digestif powers of Campari and kombucha, this drink is great before a meal, after a meal, or for sipping at your favorite comedy club or jazz club. Dial it in so that the sweet, sour, and bitter notes are balanced perfectly for your palate.

YIELD: 1 SERVING

Ice

6 ounces (175 ml) plain or flavored kombucha, such as berry, grape, or pear (see page 105 or 112)

1 shot (1½ fluid ounces, or 45 ml) of Campari, or to taste

Fill a tall glass with ice and pour the kombucha over it. Stir in the Campari and serve.

KIMCHI BLOODY MARY

The Bloody Mary cocktail as we know it today was probably created by Fernand Petiot in 1921 at the New York Bar in Paris, which later became Harry's New York Bar, a common haunt of Ernest Hemmingway.

It went through a few names, including Bucket of Blood and Red Snapper, before settling on Bloody Mary. According to one explanation, the famous spicy tomato juice and vodka cocktail was named after Queen Mary I of England whose nickname was Bloody Mary.

Another explanation of the name is that the name Bloody Mary was a mispronunciation of the name Vladimir, after Vladimir Smirnoff, whose vodka likely graced the early drinks.

Decades later, in the early 1940s, *Life* magazine described a vodka–tomato juice cocktail named the Red Hammer. This name cannot have played well once U.S. and Russia relations soured in the late 1940s!

The regular Bloody Mary has a reputation as a hangover tonic; the Kimchi Bloody Mary can only be better, since kimchi juice has significantly more vitamins and enzymes than canned, dead tomato juice.

YIELD: I SERVING

¾ cup (175 ml) kimchi juice

1 ounce (30 ml) vodka

Crushed ice

1 celery stick (optional)

Pour the kimchi juice and vodka into a large glass. Stir. Add crushed ice and a celery stick (if using) and serve.

KIMCHI MICHELADA

The Michelada is a typical Mexican alcoholic drink made with beer, sour juices, spices, and lime. You can think of it as a Bloody Mary made with beer instead of vodka. Use any beer you like, but we prefer lagers and lighter beers that aren't heavily hopped.

Like many drinks, it is said to be the perfect cure for a nasty hangover. The case for the Kimchi Michelada is stronger because of the tonic properties of fermented juice. Kimchi will give this version a spicy twist plus a shot of probiotics.

YIELD: 1 SERVING

Sea salt or worm salt (optional)

8 ounces (250 ml) beer

¼ cup (60 ml) kimchi juice

Crushed ice

Celery stick (optional)

Salt the rim of a tall glass (if salting). Add the beer and kimchi juice. Add crushed ice and a celery stick (if using). Stir.

194

SAUERKRAUT MICHELADA

For people who want to try a probiotic michelada but do not like spicy beverages, this is the perfect blend.

YIELD: 1 SERVING

Sea salt or worm salt (optional)

8 ounces (250 ml) beer

¼ cup (60 ml) sauerkraut juice

Crushed ice

Salt the rim of a tall glass (if salting). Pour in the beer and sauerkraut juice. Add crushed ice. Stir and serve.

HIBISCUS MEZCAL

As with the Kombucha Mezcal, preparing this cocktail can slowly introduce you to savoring mezcal. It is a beautifully refreshing drink for summer parties.

Pour the hibiscus soda and mezcal into a large wine glass. Add crushed ice and serve.

YIELD: 1 SERVING

8 ounces (250 ml) Hibiscus Soda (see page 128)

1 ounce (30 ml) mezcal

Crushed ice

ORANGINA MARGARITA

This is the perfect marriage between France and Mexico. It wouldn't be a proper cocktail chapter without a margarita recipe! With this probiotic margarita, you can sip guiltlessly under the sun, by the pool, or beside the ocean.

Blend the orangina, mezcal, sugar, lime juice, and ice in a blender. Pour into a tall glass and serve.

YIELD: 1 SERVING

6 ounces (175 ml) Orangina (see page 134)

1 ounce (30 ml) mezcal or tequila

1 teaspoon granulated sugar

Splash of lime juice

Ice

196

APPLE CIDER MARGARITA

It wouldn't be a proper cocktail chapter without a margarita recipe! With this probiotic margarita, you can sip guiltlessly under the sun, by the pool, or beside the ocean.

Blend the ice and all other ingredients in a blender. Pour into a margarita glass and serve.

YIELD: 1 SERVING

Ice

6 ounces (175 ml) pomegranate juice, fresh or fermented

1 ounce (30 ml) mezcal or tequila

1 teaspoon granulated sugar

Splash of lime juice

1 tablespoon (15 ml) fermented Apple Cider (see page 154)

197

APPLE CIDER BELLINI (CELLINI)

The Bellini drink was invented by the bartender Giuseppe Cipriani at Harry's Bar in Venice. The bar was opened in 1931 by Cipriani and an American named Harry Pickering. This same Cipriani that later built the Cipriani Hotel in Venice. This story was told to Raquel by Adrian Mourby, award-winning writer and producer, journalist, and hotel historian while sipping Bellinis at Harry's Bar. It was named Bellini after the famous Renaissance Italian painter Giovanni Bellini.

As I learned, Bellinis are made with only prosecco (sparkling Italian wine) and peach purée. So, we decided to introduce a new name for the cider version: Cellini. Perhaps, some day, Harry's Bar will decide to serve Cellinis.

YIELD: I SERVING

8 ounces (250 ml) sparkling wine or prosecco

1 tablespoon (15 ml) fermented Apple Cider (see page 154)

Crisp apple slices to garnish

Pour the sparkling wine into a champagne glass, add the apple cider, and garnish with the sliced apples. Serve.

GINGER ALE A LA MEXICANA

Ginger ale is not widely consumed in Mexico, but we thought that incorporating tequila or mezcal could help more people try it.

YIELD: I SERVING

Ice

8 ounces (250 ml)
Ginger Beer (see page 150)

1 ounce (30 ml)
mezcal or tequila

Splash of lime juice

Fill a tall glass with ice. Pour in the ginger beer, mezcal, and lime juice. Serve.

GINGER ALE CRANBERRY VODKA

This is a proper English-Russian mix with probiotic content and the antioxidant power of cranberries.

YIELD: I SERVING

8 ounces (250 ml)
Ginger Beer (see page 150)

4 ounces (125 ml)
cranberry juice

1 ounce (30 ml) vodka

Crushed ice

Pour the ginger beer, cranberry juice, and vodka into a tall glass. Add crushed ice and serve.

199

FOR MORE ON FERMENTING FOODS:

- *Real Food Fermentation* (Lewin)
- *The Art of Fermentation* and *Wild Fermentation* (Katz)
- Wild Fermentation: www.wildfermentation.com
- *The Art of Natural Cheesemaking* (Asher)
- The Black Sheep School of Cheesemaking: www.theblacksheepschool.com
- Cultures for Health: www.culturesforhealth.com
- *Nourishing Traditions* (Fallon)

FOR MORE ON KOMBUCHA:

- *The Big Book of Kombucha* (Crum and LaGory)
- Kombucha: The Balancing Act: http://users.bestweb.net/~om/kombucha_balance
- Kombucha Kamp: www.kombuchakamp.com
- *Kombucha—Healthy Beverage and Natural Remedy from the Far East* (Frank)

FOR MORE ON THE SCIENCE BEHIND FERMENTATION:

- *The Botany of Desire* (Pollan)
- *Gut and Psychology Syndrome* (Campbell-McBride)
- *Nutrition and Physical Degeneration* (Weston A. Price)
- "Origins of Major Human Infectious Diseases"
- *Improving Food Safety Through a One Health Approach* (Institute of Medicine)

FOR MORE ON FERMENTATION IN A CULTURAL CONTEXT:

- *Fermented Fruits and Vegetables: A Global Perspective* (Battcock and Azam-Ali)
- *Guns, Germs, and Steel* (Diamond)
- The Weston A. Price Foundation: www.westonaprice.org
- "The Worst Mistake in the History of the Human Race" *Discover* magazine, 5/2/87

TO FIND SUPPLIES:

If there's a homebrew store near you, it's worth visiting and chatting with the salespeople, who are often enthusiastic fermenters willing to field your questions. Some of the larger equipment (e.g., big jugs) are best bought in person.

- Amazon: www.amazon.com
- Craigslist: www.craigslist.org
- Kombucha Kamp: www.kombuchakamp.com
- "Raw Milk Nation," Farm-to-Consumer Legal Defense Fund: www.farmtoconsumer.org/raw-milk -nation-interactive-map
- Reddit Find a SCOBY board: http://reddit.com/r/findascoby
- Yeast Bank at White Labs: www.whitelabs.com/yeast-bank/

TO GET INVOLVED IN THE FERMENTATION COMMUNITY:

- Facebook groups: Wild Fermentation; Pura Fermentación; Kombucha Nation: Cultures, Health, and Healing!; Kombucha Kitchen Private Community; Boston Culture Sharing

ALEX LEWIN, a graduate of the Cambridge School of Culinary Arts and the Institute for Integrative Nutrition, seeks to create a healthier and tastier world by spreading the word about fermentation and real food. He teaches fermentation classes and workshops and served on the board of the Boston Public Market Association, where he helped create a year-round indoor market selling local food. He lives in Boston and San Francisco. Visit his blog at www.FeedMeLikeYouMeanIt.com.

RAQUEL GUAJARDO, a graduate of the Institute for Integrative Nutrition, runs a cooking school in Monterey, Mexico, specializing in fermentation. She also supports local, organic, and sustainable farming. She started her own brand of kombucha and fermented vegetables, which can be found in stores in several Mexican cities. Her website is www.raquelguarjardo.com.

5

FIVE-MINUTE RECIPES

69   Sweet Lassi

71   Salty or Savory Lassi

72   Doogh

73   Salty Fermented Lemonade or Limeade

74   Switchel

75   Sekanjabin

6

STARTERS, MASTER RECIPES,
AND GENERAL PRINCIPLES

83   Master Recipe: Ginger Bug

86   Master Recipe: Yogurt

88   Master Recipe: Milk Kefir

91   Master Recipe: Whey

95   Master Recipe: Vinegar

96   Master Recipe: Water Kefir

7

KOMBUCHA AND JUN

105   Kombucha, Method 1: Batch

108   Kombucha, Method 2: Continuous-Brew

111   SCOBY from Store-Bought Kombucha

112   Flavored Kombucha: Second Fermentation (2F)

113   Coffee Kombucha

114   Jun

8

VEGETABLE DRINKS

118   Beet Kvass

120   Cucumber Pickle Brine

122   Radish Brine

123   Juiced Fermented Vegetables

124   Kimchi Soda

125   Fermented Green Juice

9

SODAS

128   Hibiscus Soda

130   Grape Soda

131   Fruity Soda

132   Lemongina/Limegina

134   Orangina

135   Fruit Juice Sodas

136   Coconut Soda Kefir

12

MEXICAN PRE-HISPANIC DRINKS

175 Pulque
176 Colonche
178 Tepache
181 Tejuino

10

BEERS, GRAINS, AND ROOTS

143 Khadi (South African Beer)
144 Bread Kvass
146 Rejuvelac
148 Root(s) Beer
150 Ginger Beer

13

FERMENTED COCKTAILS

186 Ur-Piña Colada
187 Tepache Highball
188 Caliente
189 Tepache Smash
189 Kombucha Sangria
190 Kombucha Mezcal
191 Kombucha Carajillo
191 Kombucha Shandy
192 Louis CK/Kansas City
193 Kimchi Bloody Mary
194 Sauerkraut Michelada
195 Kimchi Michelada
196 Hibiscus Mezcal
196 Orangina Margarita
197 Apple Cider Margarita
198 Apple Cider Bellini
199 Ginger Ale a la Mexicana
199 Ginger Ale Cranberry Vodka

11

WINES, CIDERS, AND FRUITS (AND VINEGAR!)

154 Apple Cider 1, 2, 3
158 Perry
159 Berry Wine
161 Country Wine
162 Prison Wine/Hooch
164 Mead
166 Rice Wine
168 Sparkling Country Wine

203

INDEX

ABV (alcohol by volume), 102, 184
ABW (alcohol by weight), 184
Acerglyn, 165
Acetobacter, 79–80, 81
Acocote, 173, 174
Advertising, 11–12, 16
Agave nectar, 174
Agricultural Revolution, 29–30
Agriculture, sedentary, 29–30
Aguamiel, 173, 174
Aguamiel de maguey, 62, 63
    Pulque with milk kefir grains, 175
    Sweet Lassai, 69
    Switchel, 74
    Tepache Highball, 187
    Water Kefir, 96–97
Airlocks, for lids, 51, 53, 55, 120, 122, 155, 161, 164
Alchemy, 38
Alcohol. *See also* Cocktails
    base for herbal potions, 31
    biochemistry of fermentation and, 39–40
    Drunken Monkey hypothesis and, 28
    fermenting with a closed lid for building up, 53
    health benefits, 18, 31, 44
    home-fermented drinks lower in, 18
    in kombucha, 102
    measuring, 184
    non-industrial fermentation and, 18
    technique for getting higher levels of, 185
    in wild fermented drinks, 184
    yeasts and, 40, 78, 184
Alcohol by volume (ABV), 102, 184
Alcohol by weight (ABW), 184
Alcohol content
    ales, 142
    fractional freezing or distillation and, 185
    Ginger Beer, 150
    in kombucha, 111
    pulque, 174
    Root(s) Beer, 148
    in sodas, 129
    wild fermented drinks, 184
Alcohol production, large-scale, 18
Ales, 141, 142
Alternative medicine, 42
Amaranth, 141

Amazake, 40
Ambient air, 80
Ambient air, access to, 80–81
Ancient Greece and Rome, 30, 31, 33
Antibacterial soaps, 58, 59
Antibiotics, 24–25, 32
Ant salt, 187
"The apéritif effect," 28
Apfelwein, 154
Apple Cider Bellini, 198
Apple Cider Margarita, 197
Apple Cider Soda, 135, 154–155
Apple Cider Vinegar, 155, 157
Apple cider vinegar. *See* Raw apple cider vinegar
"Applejack," 185
Armelagos, George, 31–32
Artificial sweeteners, 62
The Art of Natural Cheese-making (Asher), 92
Asher, David, 92, 135, 175
Aspartame, 62–63
Atoms, 36–38
Autoimmune health problems, 41–42
A vitamins, 43
Aztecs, the, 33

Bacteria. *See also* Microbes
    acetobacter, 79–80, 81
    defined, 39, 78
    fermentation process and, 39
    Ginger Bug starter, 83
    kombucha and, 99, 100
    lactic-acid producing, 78
    SCOBY and, 79, 104
    war on, 24–25
    wild beers and, 141–142
Bacterial starters, 80
Barley, 141, 172
Barley wines/barleywines, 142
Batch method for kombucha, 105–107
Beer(s)
    categories of grain, 141–142
    Ginger Beer, 150–151
    growing grains and, 30
    Khadi (South African), 143
    Kimchi Michelada, 194
    Kobucha Shandy, 191
    made with *Streptyomyces* microbe, 32
    pseudo-grain ferments, 141
    Rejuvelac, 146–147

replacing pulque in Mexico, 172
Root(s) Beer, 148
Sauerkraut Michelada, 195
wine vs., 130–131
Beer Before Bread theory, 30
Beer bottles, 55, 56, 82
Beet Kvass, 118–119
Beet sugar, 63, 103
Bellini, Giovanni, 198
Berry-flavored kombucha, 118, 190
Berry Wine, 159
    Sparkling Country Wine, 168
Biochemistry, 36–40
Bio-individuality, 42
Black tea, 103
Bloody Mary, Kimchi, 193
Bob's Red Mill, 180
The Botany of Desire (Pollan), 24
Bottles, 55–56. *See also* Grolsch-style bottles; Vessels
    avoiding explosions of, 82, 97, 113, 130
    beer, 55, 56, 82
    for hibiscus soda, 129
    kombucha, 56, 82, 161
    wine, 56, 82, 159
Bottling, 56, 82
    Apple Cider Soda, 155
    Hibiscus Soda, 129
    kombucha, 107, 110, 113
Botulism, 58
BPA-free plastic bottles. *See* Plastic containers
Bread, 30, 33, 78
Bread Kvass, 144
Brine
    cucumber pickle, 120–121
    radish, 122
Brown sugar, 62, 96, 178
Buckwheat, 141, 146
Búlgaros de leche. See Milk kefir grains (*búlgaros*)
B vitamins, 14, 43, 155

Cabbage, 20, 44, 122
Caliente, 188
Camellia sinensis, 103–104
Campari, 192
Campbell-McBride, Natasha, 42
Cane sugar, 63, 96, 99, 103, 136
Cannabis, 24, 29
Canned foods, botulism and, 58

Canned fruit juice, fermented drinks vs., 45
Canning funnel, 53
Carajillo, Kombucha, 191
Carbohydrates, 38–39
Carbonation, 53, 81–82, 148, 150
Carboys, 55
Cardamom, in Sweet Lassi, 70
Carrot kvass, 119
Cassava beer, 142
Cassava root, 141
Caveat emptor, principle of, 17
Celery, 125, 193, 195
Cellini (Apple Cider Bellini), 198
Chamomile tea, 103
Champagne bottles, 82
Chapman, John, 157
Chartreuse herbal liqueur, 31
Cheesecloth, 53, 92
Cheesemaking, 91
Cheeses, molds and, 78
Chemical compound, 36
Chemical reaction, 37–38
Chemical sanitizing liquids, 59
Chloramine, 62
Chlorine, 61–62, 104
Ciders
    Apple Cider, 154–157, 197, 198
    pear (Perry), 154, 158
    Perry, 158
Cinnamon, 71, 89, 122, 148, 158, 178
Cipriani, Giuseppe, 198
Cipriani Hotel, Venice, 198
Civilization, fermentation and, 29–30
"Classic-style" kombucha, 111
Cloth handkerchiefs, 53, 57
Cloves, 120, 178
Cocktails, 183–199
    appeal of fermented beverages as, 21–22
    Apple Cider Bellini, 198
    Apple Cider Margarita, 197
    Caliente, 188
    Ginger Ale a la Mexicana, 199
    Hibiscus Mezcal, 196
    Kimchi Bloody Mary, 193
    Kimchi Michelada, 194
    Kombucha Carajillo, 191
    Kombucha Mezcal, 190
    Kombucha Sangria, 189

204

Kombucha Shandy, 191
Orangina Margarita, 196
Sauerkraut Michelada, 195
Tepache Highball, 187
Tepache Smash, 189
Ur-Piña Colada, 186
Coconut cream, 186
Coconut milk, 90, 186
Coconut Soda Kefir, 136
Coconut sugar, 62
Coconut water, 22, 90, 136, 186
Coffee, fermented drinks vs., 45
Coffee filters, 53
Coffee Kombucha, 113
Kombucha Carajillo, 191
Colonche, 176
Commercials, 11–12
Complex carbohydrates, 39, 140–141
Complex sugars, 140
Continuous-brew kombucha setup, 108–110
Cornstarch, 63
Country Wine, 161
Sparkling Country Wine, 168
Cranberry juice, 199
Crum, Hannah, 101–102
Cucumber
Cucumber Pickle Brine, 120–121
Fermented Green Juice, 125
Cumin, 71
Curry powder, 71
C vitamins, 14, 43

Dandelion root, 148
Dave, GT, 101
Dave, Laraine, 101
Demerara sugar, 62
Dextrose, 36, 39
Diamond, Jared, 30
Digestion, 12, 14
drinking water and, 20–21
health benefits of fermented drinks and, 18, 19, 44
health problems, 41
Digestive enzymes, 38
Disaccharides, 39, 101, 114, 140, 165
Dish soap, 59
Dishwasher powder, 58, 59
Doogh, 72
Dr. Hos Kombucha Beer, 102
Drinkable yogurts, 23

Drunken Monkey hypothesis, 28
The Drunken Monkey: Why We Drink and Abuse Alcohol (Dudley), 28
Dry masa flour, 180, 181
Dry yeast
Colonche, 176
Khadi, 143
Dudley, Robert, 28

Earl Grey tea, 103
Egg shells, 96
Einstein, Albert, 16
Electronic kitchen scale, 50
Elements, 36, 38
Endothermic reaction, 38
Enzymes, 12, 14, 38, 117
Equipment. See Tools and equipment
Eucharist, 33
Evolution, 28–29
Exothermic reaction, 38
Explosions, avoiding bottle, 82, 97, 113, 130

Fallon, Sally, 92, 134, 146
Fato, Ernesto, 83
Fennel seed, 71
Fermentation. See also Fermented foods and drinks; Secondary fermentation (2f)
access to ambient air for, 80–81
canning vs., 58
early history of, 28–30
explained, 12–13
human-microbe relationship and, 24–25
religion and, 33
role in health, 31–33
tools and equipment for, 47–56
Fermented coconut water, 23
Fermented foods and drinks. See also Beer(s); Kombucha; Sodas; Vegetable drinks
appeal of, 20–23
benefits of, 18
biochemistry and, 39–40
cultural continuity and, 22
health benefits of, 14, 18, 42–44
lower alcohol content in, 18–19
Mexican pre-Hispanic, 171–181

naming, 139
nutrients in, 43
other drinks vs., 43
reasons for making homemade, 23
spoilage of, 18
supporting gut microbes, 19–20
used as carriers for medicinal plants and herbs, 31
Fermented Green Juice, 125
Fermented vegetables, juiced, 123
5-minute fermented vegetable juices, 68
Fizziness, 55
Flavored kombucha, 112–113, 192
Flip-top Grolsch-style bottles, 55, 56, 112, 130, 148, 161, 168
Fly swatters, 61
Food nutrients, 14
Food of the Gods The Search for the Original Tree of Knowledge, A Radical History of Plants, Drugs, and Human Evolution (McKenna), 28
Food science, 14
Fractional distillation, 185
Fractional freezing, 185
Frank, Günther, 101
Franklin, Benjamin, 33
Fructose, 36, 39, 40, 114, 140
Fruit(s)
adding to milk kefir, 89
beers containing added, 142
Berry Wine, 159
Country Wine, 161
early ancestors eating fermented, 28
flavoring kombucha with, 112
Fruity Soda, 131
Prison Wine, 162
Sweet Lassi, 70
Fruit fly traps, 61
Fruit juices
for Fruit Juice Sodas, 135
milk kefir grains used to culture, 90
Fruit Juice Sodas, 135
Fruit wine, 154, 159
Fruity Soda, 131
Full-fat yogurt. See Plain full-fat yogurt
Funnel, canning, 53

Galactose, 36, 39
Galangal, 85, 148
GAPS diet, 101
Gases, 51
Genetically-modified (GMO) beets, 63, 103
Genetically-modified (GMO) corn, 63
Genetically-modified (GMO) masa, 180
Genetically-modified (GMO) yeasts, 18
Gin, 31, 189
Ginger
Beet Kvass, 118
Fermented Green Juice, 125
Ginger Beer, 150–151
Khadi, 143
Root(s) Beer, 148
Sekanjabin, 75
Switchel, 74
Ginger Ale, 142
Ginger Ale a la Mexicana, 199
Ginger Ale Cranberry Vodka, 199
Ginger Beer, 150–151, 188
Ginger Bug, 148
Ginger Beer, 150–151
recipe, 83–85
Glass jugs, 55
Glucose, 36, 39, 40, 114, 140
Grain beers, 141–142
Grain, sedentary agriculture and, 30
Granulated sugar, 62
Berry Wine, 159
Bread Kvass, 144
Country Wine, 161
Fruity Soda, 131
Ginger Beer, 150–151
Ginger Bug, 83
Hibiscus Soda, 128
Khadi, 143
kombucha, 99, 109, 113
Lemongina/Limegina, 132
Prison Wine, 162
Root(s) Beer, 148
Scoby, 111
Sekanjabin, 75
Sparkling Country Wine, 168
Sweet Lassi, 69
Grape cider, 154
Grape leaves, 120
Grape Soda, 130
Grapette, 130
Grasshopper salt, 187
Green apple, 125
Green tea, 103, 115

Grolsch-style bottles, 55, 56, 112, 130, 148, 161, 168
GT's Kombucha, 101, 102
Gut and Psychology Syndrome (Campbell-McBride), 42
Gut enzymes, 12, 14
Gut microbiology and health, 19, 41–42, 43

Handkerchiefs, 53, 57
Hard Apple Cider, 157
Harry's Bar, Venice, 198
Health benefits, 14, 18, 42–44
Health problems, 41–42
Hemingway, Ernest, 193
Herbal infusions, 103
Herbs and spices
    Cucumber Pickle Brine, 120
    cucumber pickle brine, 120–121
    fermented drinks used as carriers for medicinal, 31
    Flavored Kombucha, 112
    Mead, 164
    Radish Brine, 122
Hibiscus Soda
    Hibiscus Mezcal, 196
    recipe, 128–129
Holy Communion, 33
Home fermentation, benefits of, 22–23
Hominid evolution, 28–29
Honey, 62. *See also* Raw honey
    Jun and, 100, 114–115, 140
Honey mead, 140, 165
Hooch/Prison Wine, 162
    Sparkling Country Wine, 168
Hops, 141
Human saliva, 141
Hunter-gatherers, 29, 30, 41
Hygiene, excessive, 25

Immune systems, 25
Industrial chemical preservatives, 44
Industrial foods, 14, 16, 17, 18, 20
Industrial wine and beer production, 142, 184
Islam, 18–19
Isomers, 36–37, 39

"Jacking," 185
Jaggery, 62
Jars. *See also* Vessels
    covers for, 53
    for Milk Kefir, 88
    safety and sanitation when using, 58–59
    sizes of Mason, 50, 51
    with spigots, 57
    storage, 55–56
    washing, 50
Johnny Appleseed, 157
Jugs, 55–56, 59, 159, 164
Juiced Fermented Vegetables, 123
Jun, 79, 100–101, 104, 114, 140
Juniper, 31

Kale, 125
Katz, Sandor, 128
Kefir, 19, 21, 23, 45, 68, 72. *See also* Milk kefir; Water kefir (*tíbicos*)
Kefir grains. *See* Milk kefir grains (*búlgaros*); Water kefir grains
Khadi (South African Beer), 143
Kimchi, 20, 44, 68, 123
Kimchi Bloody Mary, 193
Kimchi Michelada, 194
Kimchi Soda, 124
Kombucha, 23. *See also* Jun
    alcohol content, 102
    batch method for making, 105–107
    coffee, 113
    continuous-brew method for making, 108–110
    flavored, 112–113
    ingredients for making, 103–104
    jun compared with, 114
    Kombucha Carajillo, 191
    Kombucha Mezcal, 190
    Kombucha Sangria, 189
    Kombucha Shandy, 191
    Louis CK/Kansas City, 192
    many names of, 100
    overview, 99–100
    reasons for making at home, 102
    recipe, 114–115
    rise of, 101–102
    SCOBY grown from store-bought, 111
    sugar in, 62
    supplies, 57

Kombucha bottles, 56, 82, 161
Kombucha Brewers International, 101–102
Kombucha Carajillo, 191
Kombucha: Healthy Beverage and Natural Remedy from the Far East, Its Correct Preparation and Use (Frank), 101
Kombucha Mezcal, 190
Kombucha Sangria, 189
Kombucha Shandy, 191
Kvass, 21, 23
    Beet Kvass, 118–119
    Bread Kvass, 144
K vitamins, 43

Lactic acid bacteria (LABs), 78
Lactic acid fermentation (lactofermentation), 78
Lactic acid reaction, 39
Lactose, 39, 86, 88, 90, 140
Lagers, 141
LaGory, Alex, 101–102
Lemonade, Salty Fermented, 73
Lemongina, 132
Libation, 33
Licor 43
    Kombucha Carajillo, 191
Licorice, 148
Limeade, Salty Fermented, 73
Limegina, 132
Lime juice, 134, 148, 181, 196, 197, 199
Low-alcohol beverages, 18

Maguey plant, 33, 173, 174
Make Room! Make Room! (novel), 15
Maltose, 39, 140
Mango, 70
Maple syrup, 62, 63, 140
    Acerglyn, 165
    Coconut Soda Kefir, 136
    Sweet Lassi, 69
    Switchel, 74
    Tepache Highball, 187
Maple syrup mead, 140
Mary I, Queen of England, 193
Masa dough, 180, 181
Masa harina, 181
Mason jars and lids, 50, 51, 53
    bottling with, 56
    cleaning, 59

Kombucha brewed in, 57
    safety and sanitation when using, 59
Mayahuel (goddess), 33
McKenna, Terence, 28
Mead, 65, 140, 164–165
Measuring tools, 48
Merino, Marcela, 125
Mesquite leaves, 120
Metabolism, 38
Metal strainers, 90
Methanol, 185
Metheglin, 164
Metric conversions, 50
Metric system, 48, 50
Mexican Pre-Hispanic Drinks, 171–181
    Colonche, 176
    Pulque, 172–175
    Tejuino, 181
    Tepache, 178–179
Mexican salts, 187
Mexico, 12
Mezcal
    Apple Cider Margarita, 197
    Ginger Ale a la Mexicana, 199
    Hibiscus Mezcal, 196
    Kombucha Mezcal, 190
    Orangina Margarita, 196
    Tepache Highball, 187
Michelada, 123
    Kimchi Michelada, 194
    Sauerkraut Michelada, 195
Michelson, Albert Abraham, 15–16
Microbes, 12, 14. *See also* Bacteria; Molds; Yeast(s)
    explained, 39
    fermentation and, 12, 14
    fermented drinks containing "friendly," 43
    gut, 19–20
    gut enzymes and, 12, 14
    in the human organism, 20
    human relationship with, 24–25
    in whey, 91
Microbial diversity, 20, 23
Milk
    fermented drinks vs., 45
    for making yogurt, 86
Milk kefir, 79, 88–90, 89, 92
Milk kefir grains (*búlgaros*), 79, 88
    distinguished from coagulated milk, 90
    Fruit Juice Sodas, 135
    Orangina, 134

pulque with, 175
used to culture coconut water, coconut milk, fruit juices, and nut milks, 90
Minerals, 63–64
Mint leaves, 72, 73, 75
Mint tea, 103
Molasses, 62, 63, 74, 96, 187
Molds, 39, 40, 78
Molecules, 36
Monkeys, 28
Monosaccharides, 39, 101, 114, 140
Mormons, 18
Mother of vinegar, 79
Mourby, Adrian, 198
Muscovado, 62

Nelson, Mark, 32
New York Times article on kombucha, 101
Nourishing Traditions (Fallon), 92, 134
Nubian bones, 31–32
Nut milks, milk kefir grains used to culture, 90
Nutrients, 14, 15, 23, 43, 44, 184
Nutrition, 15–17

Oak leaves, 120, 122
Oil of bergamot, 103
Oligosaccharides, 39
Oolong tea, 103
Opioids, 12
Orange juice, 134, 135
Orangina, 134
Orangina Margarita, 196

Panela sugar, 62, 96, 136, 178, 181
Paracelsus, 44
Passover seder, 33
Pathogenic microbes, 18, 43, 44
Pear cider, 154, 158
Pear soda, 158
Perry, 154, 158
Personal care products, 17
Petiot, Fernand, 193
Phosphoric acid, 21, 142
Phytic acid, 44, 63
Pickles, 68, 120–121
Piloncillo sugar, 62, 96, 172, 181
Piña Colada, 22

Pineapple
Khadi, 143
Sweet Lassi, 70
Tepache, 178–179
Tepache Highball, 187
tips and tricks, 179
Pineapple corer, 179
Pineapple tepache vinegar, 74
Plain full-fat yogurt
bacterial starters, 80
Doogh, 72
for five-minute recipes, 68
for making whey, 91
Salty or Savory Lassi, 71
Sweet Lassi, 69
whey recipe, 91–92
Planck, Max, 16
Plastic containers, 55, 82
for Apple Cider Soda, 155
bottling kombucha in, 107, 113
for fruit juice sodas, 135
for Ginger Beer, 150
for Hibiscus Soda, 129
for Pulque, 175
Plastic siphon pumps, 56
Plastic spigots, 57
Pollan, Michael, 24
Polysaccharides, 39
Pomegranate juice, 197
Posca, 31
Powdered sugar, 63
Preservatives, 44, 65, 141, 154
Prickly pear, 131, 176
Prison Wine, 162
Probiotic supplement pills, 43
Processed foods, 14, 20
Proof, 184
Prosecco, 198
Proteins, 38
Psilocybin mushrooms, 29
Pulque, 142, 172–175
Pulquerías, 172

The Quarterly Review of Biology, 28
Quince juice, 158
Quinoa, 141, 146

Radish Brine, 122
Raisins, 96, 144
Rapadura sugar, 96
Raspberries, 132
Raw apple cider vinegar, 23, 68, 74, 157
Rawdelicious, 125
Raw fruit juice, fermented drinks vs., 45

Raw honey
dissolving in warm water, 68
Mead, 164–165
Salty Fermented Lemonade/Limeade, 73
Sweet Lassi, 69
Switchel, 74
Raw milk
Milk Kefir, 88
whey made with, 92
Raw sauerkraut, 68
Raw sugar, 62
Raw wheat berries, 146
Real Food Fermentation, 68
Real foods, 14–17
Red wine, 189
Refrigeration, 58, 74, 82, 92, 97, 113, 119
Regulators, of food, 16–17
Rejuvelac, 146–147
Religion, fermentation and, 33
Rhizomes, 148
Rice ferments, 40
Rice Wine, 166–167
Rice wine yeast ball, 166
Rooibos tea, 103
Root beer, 21, 142, 148
Rosemary, 118, 164
Rum, 186
Rye bread, 144

Saccharine, 62
Safety and sanitation equipment, 58–59
Sal de Chapulín (grasshopper salt), 187
Sal de Guano (worm salt), 187, 194, 195
Sal de Hormiga (ant salt), 187
Saliva, human, 141
Salty Fermented Lemonade or Limeade, 73
Sangria, Kombucha, 189
Sassafras root bark, 148
Sauerkraut, 21, 44, 68, 123, 125
Sauerkraut juice, 195
SCOBY, 79. *See also* Water kefir grains
Jun, 115
kombucha, 104, 107, 109
starters, 79–80
from store-bought kombucha, 111
Sealed containers, 82
Secondary fermentation (2f), 56, 82, 89
beer, 142

Coconut Soda Kefir, 136
Flavored Kombucha, 112–113
Grape Soda, 130
Sparkling Country Wine, 168
Sekanjabin, 75
Shanghai yeast ball, 166
Shōchū, 40
Shrub, 23
Simple sugars, 39, 140
Singapore, 102
Siphoning, 155, 159, 161
Siphon pumps, 55–56, 59
Soda Chanh, 73
Sodas, 127–136
appeal of fermented drinks imitating, 21
Coconut Soda Kefir, 136
fermented drinks vs., 45
Fruit Juice Sodas, 135
Fruity Soda, 131
Grape Soda, 130
Hibiscus Soda, 128–129
kimchi, 124
Lemongina/Limegina, 132
Orangina, 134
Soju, 40
Sourdough starter, 144, 145
Soylent, 14–15
Soylent Green (film), 15
Sparkling Country Wine, 168
Sparkling water
Doogh, 72
fermented vegetable juices with, 68
kimchi soda, 124
Switchel served with, 74
Sparkling wine, 198
Spearmint leaf, 118
Spices. *See* Herbs and spices
Spinach, 125
Spoilage, of fermented foods, 18
Sports drinks, fermented drinks vs., 45
Standards American Diet (SAD), 20
Star anise, 178
Starches, 140–141
Starters
bacterial, 80
explained, 79
Ginger Bug, 83
SCOBY, 79–80
sourdough, 145
whey used as, 87, 91–92
yeast, 80
Sticky rice, 166
Stoned Ape theory, 28–29
Strainers, 53, 90

207

Straining
    dairy yogurt, 92
    milk kefir, 90
    water kefir grains, 90, 97, 134
Streptomyces microbe, 32
Sucanat, 62
Sucralose, 62
Sucrose, 36, 39, 114, 140
Sugar. *See* Cane sugar; Granulated sugar
Super Bowl commercials, 12
Supplements, probiotic, 43
Sweeteners. *See also* individual types of sweeteners
    for Coconut Soda Kefir, 136
    for kombucha, 100–101
    for Salty Fermented Lemonade or Limeade, 73
Sweet Lassi, 69
Switchel, 21, 23, 74

Tannins, 120
Tea
    fermented drinks vs., 45
    used for kombucha, 103–104
Tepache, 22, 40, 80
    Caliente, 188
    recipe, 178–179
    Tepache Highball, 187
    Tepache Smash, 189
    Ur-Piña Colada, 186
Tequila
    Apple Cider Margarita, 197
    Ginger Ale a la Mexicana, 199
    Orangina Margarita, 196
Tetracycline, 32
Thucydides, 30
Tíbicos. See Water kefir (*tíbicos*)
Tlachiquero, 173, 174
Tools and equipment
    for bottling, 56
    filtered water, 61–62
    fly swatters, 61
    fruit fly traps, 61
    jars, 50–53
    for kombucha, 57
    kombucha, continuous-brew setup, 108–109
    measuring, 48
    for safety and sanitation, 58–59

storage bottles/jars, 55–56
sugar, 62–65
Traditional soju, 40
Triclosan, 59
Tulips, 24
Turbinado sugar, 62, 96
Turmeric, 71, 85
2f (secondary fermentation). *See* Secondary fermentation (2f)

Unfiltered fermented drinks, 43, 184
Unfiltered vinegar, 74, 75
Unrefined sugar, 63
Ur-Piña Colada, 186
U.S. customary units, 48

Vanilla bean/vanilla extract, 89, 148
Vegetable drinks, 117–125
    Beet Kvass, 118–119
    Cucumber Pickle Brine, 120–121
    Fermented Green Juice, 125
    Juiced Fermented Vegetables, 123
    Kimchi Soda, 124
    Radish Brine, 122
Vegetable fermentation starters, 80
Vermouth, 31
Vessels. *See also* Bottles; Mason jars and lids
    bottling in serving-sized, 82
    for Kombucha, 57
    Mason jars and lids, 50–53
    old, "teaching" the new, 36
    safety and sanitation for using, 58–59
    sealing, 81
    for storage, 55–56
Villa de Patos brand of maguey sap, 174
Vinegar
    Apple Cider Vinegar, 155–156
    drinking water with, 31
    making homemade, 959
    not needing a starter, 79–80
    watered-down, 31
    when to use homemade vs. store-bought, 95
Viruses, 12

Vitamins, 14, 43, 155
Vodka
    Ginger Ale Cranberry Vodka, 199
    Kimchi Bloody Mary, 193

"War on bacteria," 24–25
Water
    for brewing tea for kombucha, 104
    chlorine in, 61–62
    drinking too much, 20–21
    drinking with vinegar, 31
    fermented drinks vs., 45
    filtering, 62, 104
    impurities in, 61–62
    mixing with wine, 31
    removing impurities from, 61–62
Water kefir (*tíbicos*), 79, 140
    Grape Soda, 130
    recipe, 96–97
Water kefir grains, 96, 136
Weight gain/loss, 41
Wheat, 78, 141, 172
Wheat berries, 146
Wheat bran, 143
Whey
    cheesemaking and, 91
    Lemongina/Limegina, 132
    Orangina, 134
    recipe, 91–92
    Root(s) Beer, 148
    used as a starter, 87, 91–92
White vinegar, 58, 59, 75
WHO Model List of Essential Medicines, 32
Wild fermented drinks, 184. *See also* Fermented foods and drinks
Wild yeast grain beers, 141–142
Wild yeasts
    air and, 80–81
    beer and, 141–142
    benefits of home-fermented drinks and, 18
    Berry Wine, 159
    sourdough starter and, 145
    wine and, 31
Wine(s)
    additives in, 153
    Apple Cider Bellini (Cellini), 198
    beer vs., 140–141
    Berry Wine, 159
    Country Wine, 161

fruit, 155
Kombucha Sangria, 189
mixing with water, 31
Prison Wine/Hooch, 162
Rice Wine, 166–167
role in Judaic tradition, 33
Sparkling Country Wine, 168
vinegar made from, 95
Wine bottles, 56, 82, 95, 159, 162
Wine yeast, 159
Wintergreen leaf, 148
"Wood alcohol," 185
Wooden barrel, 57
Wood spigots, 57
World Health Organization (WHO), 32, 41
Worm salt, 187, 194, 195
"Wormwood," 31
"The Worst Mistake in the History of the Human Race" (Diamond), 30

Yeast(s). *See also* Dry yeast; Microbes
    alcohol and, 40, 78, 184
    Apple Cider sediment and, 155
    beer vs. wine and, 140
    defined, 39
    explained, 78
    genetically-modified, 18
    kombucha and, 99, 100
    nutrients in, 43
    SCOBY and, 79, 104
    starches and, 140
    wild, 18, 80, 140, 142, 184
    wild beers and, 141–142
Yeast reaction, 40
Yeast starters, 80
Yogurt. *See also* Plain full-fat yogurt
    kefir and, 88
    microbial diversity and, 23
    recipe, 86–87
    starter necessary for, 80
    straining dairy, 92